Sacred Soul Love

Manifesting True Love and Happiness by Revealing and Healing Blockages and Limitations

Dr. Lisa Thompson

Life, Love & Soul Coach specializing in
Past Life Regression and Human Design

Mystic Manta Publishing
Olympia, WA

Cover design by: Transcendent Publishing
Interior design by: Transcendent Publishing
Author portrait by: Ben Leavitt

ISBN: 978-1-7324088-1-4

www.MysticManta.com

Dedication

This book is dedicated to all the women out there struggling to find and keep love. It is for my amazing, talented, intelligent girlfriends who have been married, divorced and are now trying to find their next love chapter of real enduring love. It is for the women who have stayed in loveless marriages for the sake of the children. It is for the women who yearn for love because they have never experienced it.

"The only thing we never get enough of is love;
and the only thing we never give enough of is love."
— **Henry Miller**

Contents

Acknowledgments

This book could not have been written without the help and support of my friends, family and mentors.

I want to thank Shanda Trofe, who coached me in putting this book together.

I am grateful to my amazing and patient husband, Skip Thompson, and my two children, Nohwa and Curran, for supporting me in writing this book and loving me through it.

I have gratitude for my mother for introducing me to the spiritual journey I have been on in this life.

And finally, I am thankful for all the love relationships, good and bad, throughout my life that have led me to find my true love and happiness.

1

Introduction to Sacred Soul Love

> *"Life without love is like a tree*
> *without blossoms or fruit."*
> — **Khalil Gibran**

I was thirty years old when it happened. The man I was in a relationship with had pinned me to the floor and twisted my arm behind my back, threatening to break it. I don't even remember what caused the argument. What I do remember is his face as it looked down at me - bright red and demonic, as if he was possessed.

Though my body was paralyzed by fear, my mind was racing. How could I be here? Why is this happening to me? How had I gotten in so deep? I tried unsuccessfully to get out of his stronghold, then was filled with relief when he abruptly let me go before the bone snapped. You would think this would have been my wakeup call to end the relationship. It wasn't. This was the beginning of my nightmare.

I woke up the next morning still not able to wrap my mind around what happened. I was used to other types of abuse in my relationships, mostly emotional, though I wasn't aware of this while I was in them, but never had anyone put his hands on me. In fact, I thought I, an intelligent woman with a PhD, was above such things. This happened to other women, not me. I had even secretly judged those abused women. How could they allow such cruelty? Why didn't they just pick up and leave?

Of course there had been signs. About a month earlier, my cats had gone missing. They had always been afraid of him, shaking uncontrollably every time he came to the house. He hated them too; he hated all cats. After they disappeared I found out he had taken them to the woods. He told me he had shot them in their cages, then later changed his story and said he just set them free. However, he had also told some of our friends that he had killed them, which made me believe it did happen. As devastated as I was, I still didn't believe he would turn his rage on me… until he nearly broke my arm.

Over the next few years, the cycle of abuse continued, rage followed by his pleas for forgiveness and efforts to redeem himself. Most of the abuse was emotional and verbal, but, there were times, in addition to the arm incident, when it got physical. Sometimes, it was the threat of violence to my person, like when he threw all of my dishes against the wall. Our bedroom was next to the kitchen, and I was lying in bed. Broken shards of pottery came flying into the room, almost hitting me. I laid there paralyzed, pretending to be asleep, afraid of what he would do to me if he knew I was awake. A year or so later, he threatened to break all of my new dishes because he wanted to keep me in fear, under his control. There were times I thought I had caused his anger and deserved the abuse. Mostly, though, I was in a state of shock. I didn't know what to do or how to get out of it.

One of my greatest fears was what I would do for a job if I left him. I had already changed careers once, which wasn't easy, and I couldn't imagine having to start all over again. Further complicating matters was the fact that we had a business together, one my family and friends had invested in. If I left him, everything we were building would collapse. With darkness closing in around me, I became the martyr and accepted my lot in life.

The week before our wedding, I found out I was pregnant with my first child. I wanted a baby badly, and I had hopes he would change for the sake of the child. He didn't. He became even more dangerous. My aunt came to me when I was six months pregnant, telling me she was worried he would kill me one day. As a volunteer at Safe Place for years, she knew the signs of an abusive spouse.

After nearly five years in this relationship, I gave him an ultimatum about how he was treating me. He promised he would be different, only to cross the line again a few months later. Now was my moment to fight for myself and my seven-month-old baby girl. I didn't want her to grow up thinking this is how a man treats a woman. If I couldn't leave him for me, then I had to do it for her. With the help of friends and family, I finally ended the relationship.

Second Marriage a Bust

During the divorce from my first husband, I met the man who would become husband number two. Nice, kind and affectionate, he seemed to be the opposite of what I had just escaped. As our relationship progressed, I discovered how subtly undermining he could be, but it was too late. Five months in I found out I was pregnant. Though I knew we hadn't been together long enough to become parents, I didn't want my daughter to be an only child. I also thought this might be my last opportunity of having a healthy baby, as at age thirty-five I was considered a "geriatric mother" by the doctors.

Still, I had hope that things would work out. Like many relationships, ours began with a lot of physical touch and affection, which was different from my first marriage. Once the baby came, however, things changed. We went long periods of having no intimacy, sometimes up to six months. When we were in an argument, we would occasionally go a week or two without speaking to each other. It was not healthy. We were more roommates than lovers.

Had we not gotten pregnant, it's possible I would have realized that this was not the man I wanted to be with. Then again, maybe I wouldn't have. When I met him, I was at the bottom of the barrel; I judged myself harshly for having been in the abusive relationship with my first husband; I had little self-worth and I certainly did not love myself. I also didn't know how to love anyone else after what I had just been through.

All told, I would spend eight rocky years with my second husband. He wasn't abusive like my previous husband, but I felt powerless. I was not allowed to be authentic. He was afraid of my spiritual side and wanted to control what kind of information I shared with the children. We spent nearly two years in couple's therapy before I agreed to marry him, and even when I did it was not without reservations. The tiny voice in my head was telling me not to, but I ignored it, mostly because I thought it was the right thing to do for my kids.

When I decided to leave my second marriage, I knew it was time to take stock of my life and make some changes to the way I had been living it. I was forty-two years old with two ex-husbands and two children with two different dads. I also thought about my mother, my aunt and my grandmother, all of whom had divorced their husbands and never had successful relationships afterwards, and decided I didn't want to be like them. I wanted to share my life with a partner who would reciprocate my love and experience the joys of life to the maximum; I also wanted to be the role model of love and healthy relationships for my children. In order to do this, however, I would first have to heal myself.

Learning to Love Myself

"Every person has to love at least one bad partner in their lives to be truly thankful for the right one."
— **Unknown**

To be able to attract and marry the love of my life, I had to fall in love with myself. First, though, I had to acknowledge I didn't currently love myself, and that I didn't know how to have a healthy relationship. Until that point, I had thought my relationships didn't work out because they were just not the right person for me. The truth was, I was the common denominator in all of those relationships. *I* was not the right person for me. And if I wasn't right for me, they couldn't be either.

In order to heal, I got back in touch with my long-neglected spiritual side, using tools I had learned over the years to dig deep and find the wounds that were keeping me from attracting true love. I learned how to come to terms with my familial relationships and the stories that went along with them. Pain runs deep in my ancestral bloodline, and like most people I had internalized my family members' ideas and beliefs about relationships. I grew up searching for love wherever I could find it. I felt incomplete, insecure and unlovable. I tried to be the perfect child with the perfect grades so I would get attention and feel worthy and loved. These feelings had led to three decades of unhealthy relationships with boyfriends and twelve years of toxic marriages. In order to heal, I had to stop making all of those relationships wrong and understand that I was in them to learn valuable lessons.

It took almost a year for me to get to a place where I could say I loved myself. My life improved; I was having fun with friends, traveling, making money and calling my own shots. I was rising as the phoenix from the ashes, owning my power. I was free.

Four years later, I am still doing the work to go even deeper, but now it is from a place of wholeness and observation, rather than judgment and victimhood. Once I embraced my self-love and worthiness, I met the love of my life. Our relationship is like none other than I have ever experienced. It is filled with friendship, respect, trust, compassion, and love. We resonate together on the highest frequency. We are an inspiration to our friends and family members. We continue to cultivate the Soul Love and happiness we share on a daily basis. Last year we committed our lives to each other in a wedding ceremony in Thailand, a dream come true.

Sacred Soul Love

Sacred Soul Love must start with the purest love of oneself. Without self-love, there is no true love, for we can only have what we are.

Much of what we are at any given time is determined by patterns – some we have created and others that have been handed to us by our family and/or society. The good news is that while these patterns can be challenging to break, once we do we can step into a better version of ourselves. We become the most important person in our lives. We know who we are. We know what we want and need. We give it to ourselves. From this place as a whole person, we can then merge our lives with other whole people while staying true to ourselves.

When we heal ourselves, we don't keep attracting the same kind of toxic relationship over and over in new packaging. We can see through the words and actions of others in our lives. We can hear and feel the truth. We don't allow anything less than loving truth into our lives. If we experience something that doesn't fit with our new reality, we take notice of it and remove it. Even if the person we are involved with isn't quite whole and healthy, we can maintain our energetic boundary and stay whole within our sphere. We realize that love is not co-dependent. Love does not want to fix. Love wants to be with love. Love understands we are all human living a human experience and are therefore not perfect.

Before falling in love with myself, I didn't feel worthy of love from a partner. I compared myself to others. I pretended to be something I wasn't. I was jealous and competitive. I was fearful and anxious. I had abandonment issues. I allowed myself to be treated like garbage and disrespected.

What I am here to tell you is you can find true love, and it all starts with finding love for yourself, unconditionally.

What to Expect from This Book

If you're reading this book, you've probably realized that you have a pattern of attracting unhealthy relationships and want to break it. As you go through it, however, you may realize that your life begins to change on several fronts. Why? Because, as mentioned earlier, a lack of loving relationships with others is an indicator that we do not have a loving relationship with ourselves.

When we don't love ourselves it is very difficult to achieve balance, not just romantically, but in every aspect of life. Finances are a good example of this; if you don't love yourself, you might be overspending on clothes, beauty products and even plastic surgery or other medical procedures to alter your physical appearance. You also might be paying for online dating with no results. Emotionally, you might be stuck in a pattern of boredom and loneliness where you don't feel worthy of love. Your physical health may be suffering as well, leading to dis-ease and possibly shortening your life. Therefore, it is my goal to assist you in learning to love yourself, not only so you can attract a healthy, loving partner, but the life you want.

Wherever you find yourself at this moment, the first thing to understand is that it is not your fault. We all learn things – about relationships and life in general - from our parents and other family members. We all have genetic memory in our DNA from our ancestral bloodline. We make up stories about our experiences throughout life and the relationships we have.

We can change all of this; to do so, however, we must uncover our beliefs, blocks and limitations. Only when we do this can we heal those wounds and change our patterns. Our desire to change and have a better life has to be stronger than our comfort of staying in our pain. We need to change the environment we are immersed in and create a new environment that emotionally, physically and spiritually supports us in love.

Throughout this book, I will take you through the processes I did and continue to do in order to reveal my wounds and heal myself from them so I could become a whole and healthy person. If you do them faithfully, you too will learn to pull back the layers so that you can find and heal your wounds. You will begin to see that your experiences, as painful as they were, provided you with valuable lessons that brought you to where you are today. You will begin to transform your life in ways you might not have believed possible.

Are you ready to begin your personal transformation, to be that phoenix rising from the ashes? Let's get started.

"Keep love in your heart. A life without it is like a sunless garden when the flowers are dead."
— Oscar Wilde

2

Examining Relationship History

"We accept the love we think we deserve."
— **Stephen Chbosky,** *The Perks of*
Being a Wallflower

When it comes to love relationships, finding and cultivating healthy relationships proves to be more challenging than we think it will be when we are growing up. From early childhood, we are fed the story of happily ever after in the movies we watch and the books we read. What we don't learn from these stories is how to cultivate healthy, true love, or how to maintain it. Why? Because these fanciful stories usually do not go beyond the part where the couple falls in love, though this is actually where the real work begins.

Since the age of three, I have been searching for my happily ever after. As mentioned earlier, my journey to find it was fraught with several unhealthy and toxic relationships, some of which I will share in this chapter. In addition to my own learning experiences, I have observed my friends, family and acquaintances go through some very tough situations. As I write this, some of them are still living out this vicious cycle. Like most of us, they are not always conscious of the situations they are in. As one of my spiritual teachers told me, "When you are red in the rainbow, you can't see the color red."

When I was in my abusive marriage, I didn't see myself as abused until I started seeing it in other couples and noticed my situation was similar. I started believing friends and family who approached me with their concerns about my partner. It took years. It is my hope that in sharing some of my experiences, someone will recognize themselves and see the need to leave the relationship. If while reading this, emotions come up, that's great. This is part of the revealing process, and the first step to healing.

How we do relationships has everything to do with how our mind is wired. Remember, our issues may come from our parents, our ancestors, experiences with significant others, or, most likely, a combination of all of these. They even come from past lives, resulting in residual karmic energy that needs to be completed. Whatever the reason, we can reveal the wound and heal it to change our current and future reality.

We will begin to uncover the roots of unhealthy relationships with exercises geared towards examining patterns in our lives. We will look at parental and ancestral belief systems, as well as early relationships and possible past lives. This will give us a starting point to peel back the layers to get to the core of our inner self.

Unhealthy Relationships

In this section, I describe some of the different types of unhealthy and toxic relationships I have witnessed in others. Names may have been changed to protect the identity of these individuals.

Serial Relationships

Laura's story

Laura is an intelligent, successful woman in her forties who has been divorced for twelve years. During that time she has had one boyfriend after another. She "falls in love" easily, seeing their greatest potential and hoping they will live up to her vision. In one way or another, however, they have not been the right match for her. Before she breaks up with one boyfriend, she usually has another one lined up. She recently had one significant relationship that lasted six years, but she realized she was the one carrying the relationship and decided she couldn't do it anymore. Her longest time between boyfriends is about one month. As she is getting older, she's tired of being on the hamster wheel of serial dating and ready to find her perfect match to live her happily ever after.

Attracting Mr. Wrong

Christie's story

Christie is a successful woman and full of fun. She met her ex-husband in high school, married very young and immediately had two children. Their marriage, which was unhealthy and toxic, ended after eighteen years. In the several years since the divorce, Christie continues to attract the wrong men through online dating and when she is out at the bar. The men she meets don't respect her, but treat her like a "booty call" or someone to spend time with when it is convenient or they are bored. Christie is ready to meet Mr. Right.

Anne's story

Anne is a divorced woman with a young heart. After her divorce, she would date men based on initial chemistry, rather than getting to know them to see if they were compatible. After a three-year relationship with a nice man who had little in common with her, she went online to find dates. Being beautiful and spunky, she attracted lots of attention from the online world, but the majority of them were quite a bit younger and saw her as a hookup rather than relationship material. She too based her interest first and foremost on appearance and didn't understand why she was not finding love. It has taken her a long time, but she now realizes the reason she was attracting the same kind of man over and over. She is still looking for The One.

Abusive Relationship

Shauna's story

Shauna is a single mom in her forties who has never been married. She's a beautiful woman who is nevertheless filled with insecurities, usually around her looks. She works out religiously, she's had breast enlargement, and she regularly gets Botox and other enhancements done to her face. Because of her self-worth issues, she tends to seek out physically attractive men who aren't necessarily the nicest of people. In the last several years, she has had multiple boyfriends who cheat on her, ignore her and abuse her. Recently she got engaged to a man with anger issues who regularly abuses her emotionally, verbally and physically. Her desire for love overrides her better judgment to get away from this latest "bad guy."

Laurie's story

Laurie found herself married to an alcoholic. When he was sober, he was sweet and loving. When he was drinking, he was emotionally and verbally abusive. They had two young children together. One day Laura realized she could not let her children grow up in such an unhealthy and unhappy home. They deserved better, and so did she.

Loveless Marriage

Sheri's story

Sheri has been married to the same man for twenty-three years. They have a child together who is getting ready to go off to college. Sheri now realizes she and her husband will be alone in the house without the distraction of the child. She doesn't have anything in common with her husband. He is an angry man whose values and life views are very different from hers. She doesn't love him anymore, and she knows he is unable or unwilling to change. She must decide if she is going to stay in the marriage and develop herself despite him, or if she is going to leave him to find a life of joy. She is fearful of the unknown.

Larry's story

Larry has been married to his second wife for seventeen years. During this time, they have grown apart and now just tolerate each other. They mostly spend their time separately doing activities with their other friends and family members rather than being with each other. Larry has wanted to leave her for the last three years, but he hasn't brought himself to do it out of fear and complacency.

Codependent

Anita's story

Anita is a high achiever who goes above and beyond in her relationships with men. One example is her most recent boyfriend. When they met, he was working a minimum wage job as he had just moved to her town and was trying to build a new life for himself. For her, it was lust at first sight. After a few months he moved in with her, and shortly after that, she employed him at her company. Over the next several years, she worked to help him transform into the man she wanted him to be. Ultimately the power imbalance became too much and he decided he didn't want to work for her anymore. On the other hand, he never gained employment elsewhere and was content to live off her. He also wasn't doing his equal share of the chores around the household, leaving Anita to pick up the slack in addition to being the breadwinner. She spent a lot of money helping him heal an illness, paid for his plastic surgery to remedy a body image issue that he struggled with, and bought him expensive "toys," including a boat and an off-road vehicle. She was his sugar mama, and he loved it. One day she decided she was done giving so much without receiving anything in return.

Parental & Ancestral relationships

When we begin to look at our patterns of love relationships in our lives, it is important to see the love story running in the back of our minds. We come into life in particular familial situations, with no conscious control over the ideas and beliefs that we internalize. These range from things we observe or are told outright, to things we energetically pick up, such as how our parents felt when we were in the womb or are genetically passed down through our ancestral bloodline. Either way, they eventually become our own and lead to patterns and behaviors that shape our love relationships.

The first step in being able to change these patterns and behaviors is to determine the root cause of those issues. In this section, I share my story of familial relationships to show you some of the early seeds planted in my mind that led to having toxic relationships. I include exercises to help you examine your own parental and ancestral relationships.

My story

My parents met and started dating while in high school. They broke up when my mom and her family moved out of state, then reunited a couple of years later and got married when my mom was twenty and my dad was twenty-two. According to the stories I've heard, they had a rocky marriage and after five years were on the verge of divorce when I was conceived. They had attended my aunt's wedding and I guess love was in the air.

I don't think my mom ever really wanted kids, but there I was – a new life she had to take care of. I'm not quite sure how my dad felt about my arrival. They tried to work out their relationship for my sake but ended up getting divorced when I was two years old.

While I don't have clear memories of those first two years of life, I know I had constant earaches, which led to me getting tubes in my ears. There was a lot of fighting in the house.

After the divorce, my mom and I moved to Oklahoma City to be close to my aunt and her husband. My dad moved to Lincoln, Nebraska to help his father run his sporting goods store.

It was only after having my own kids that I understood how hard it was for my mom to be a single, working parent of a two-year-old. She did everything she could to build a life for herself. In my early years she worked a lot and rose up through the ranks of the company. Nights and weekends she spent at astrology classes and also went to college, receiving her bachelor's degree in psychology when I was in the fifth grade. When she wasn't doing those things she was dating, which, coupled with her other pursuits, left very little time for me. I learned at an early age to entertain myself. I spent hours drawing animals, reading, playing with barbies and playing board games by myself. I was lonely. And bored.

I saw my dad twice a year, once in the summer, and once at either Thanksgiving or Christmas. For the first two years after the divorce, all of our time on these visits was spent together. He would make the eight-hour drive from Lincoln to Oklahoma City to pick me up, then we would head back to Lincoln together, only to reverse the process when it was time for me to return home.

When I was four, Dad met the woman who was to become my stepmom. Also around that time, my parents decided to have me fly back and forth rather than doing the long drive. I flew from Oklahoma City to Kansas City, where my father would pick me up at the airport. The three-hour drive to Lincoln became the only quality time we had.

My stepmom was a teacher, which meant she had summers and holidays off. I spent more time with her than I did my dad during the visits. Oftentimes, the only alone time we had were one or two lunch dates.

When I was seven, my stepmom gave birth to twin boys, which further changed the family dynamic during my visits. The distance between me and my dad was growing larger each year. I didn't realize the effect it would have on my future relationships until I was in my mid-thirties and going through my first divorce.

When I was home with my mom, my dad would not call to talk to me. My stepmom was the one who always reached out. She bought the birthday and Christmas gifts. She wrote and mailed the child support checks. He had delegated his parenting to her.

When I did speak to him, I heard not loving words, but a lot of criticism. I wasn't pretty enough; I wasn't athletic enough. As a teenager I became a very good dancer, but for him dancing wasn't good enough. He owned a sporting goods store and expected me to enjoy and be talented at sports like he and my brothers were. He only vaguely appreciated my talents years later, when one of my brothers dated a girl on the high school dance team. The biggest compliment I ever got from my dad was when I received my PhD. He told me I had done a really good job raising myself. I couldn't argue with him. He was right.

My mom was not the touchy-feely type. She rarely gave affection, said only an occasional "I love you," and was not good at communicating her feelings and emotions with me. When I was around five or six, I got lost a couple of different times in stores we were shopping in and had huge fear that she would leave me behind. As a child, these experiences, compounded the feelings of abandonment by my dad, led me to become a perfectionist, needing to get excellent grades so I could get the attention I was craving. As an adult, it led to anxiety and fear in my relationships.

That said, I don't fault my mother for this, as I now fully understand her journey with her own parents while growing up. What I had to learn is you can't go to the hardware store for milk. My mother was the metaphorical "hardware store."

In my teen years, I spent most of my time with friends and boyfriends. Since my mother was hands-off, it was easy for me to lie to her about where I was and who I was with. Thus began my double life – by day, I was a straight A student and captain and choreographer of the dance team who worked twenty to twenty-five hours a week. On nights and weekends, I was out partying with my friends and boyfriends, sometimes staying out all night at random people's homes where the party or after-party was. When Mom finally caught me I was in my junior year of high school and so independent I told her if she didn't think she had done a good job raising me it was too late.

By the time I went to college I was ready to disown both of my parents. I had received a full ride scholarship to school, so they weren't paying for it. I didn't feel like I needed them anymore because I really had been on my own for so long.

When I was nineteen, I wrote my dad a letter saying I didn't need him in my life anymore, as he had not been there for me. Around the same time, my mom attended a self-help seminar series and came back from her weekend apologizing to me for my childhood. She then paid for me to go to the seminar so I could start dealing with issues related to her and my father. That was my first real experience in looking inside myself to heal. It was also the beginning of a nearly twenty-five-year journey into finding the love deep inside me.

Growing up feeling ignored and less important than other people and situations did a number on my psyche and how I viewed myself in the world. What I was good at was compartmentalizing my emotions and not letting them distract me from doing the things I was good at, including dance and school. I was a high-functioning perfectionist but damaged on the inside.

My childhood trauma led to different health issues throughout my life, which I cover in more detail in the next chapter. These included asthmas attacks, allergic reactions to the sun and grass and tonsillitis, as well as random ear problems. In graduate school, I developed a serious psoriasis outbreak that covered my entire body and lasted six months.

When I look back on my growing up years, the most frequent emotions I felt were those of being unlovable, unworthy, lonely, bored, and abandoned. I also heard from my female relatives that men were "bad" or dangerous, and not to trust them or depend on them. There was little physical touch of hugging and kissing in my family, and the words "I love you" were rarely used as well. These are the things I sought out in my love relationships.

Exercise 2.1: Write Your Story About Your Relationship with Your Parents

Think about your story of the relationships you had with your parents. Write your story with as much detail as you can. You may wish to do this here, write it in a journal or type it on your computer, whatever is best for you. This process will help you uncover the stories and beliefs in your mind related to your parents.

Ancestral Relationships

Once we understand how we grew up and the ideas we were taught, we can go back further in the family line to see what was going on with our parents as they were growing up.

On my mother's side, there is a long family history of not having self-love. I began to understand these patterns due to a series of identical health issues that popped up in several family members.

When my maternal granddaddy was sixty-five, he died of a heart attack. When my mother, who is the oldest child in her family, turned sixty-five, she too had a heart attack but was able to recover from it. My uncle, my mom's younger brother, died at the age of sixty-five from a heart attack and stroke. My aunt, the youngest girl in the family had a heart attack at sixty-five, and so far has survived, though not without major medical intervention in the way of a permanent heart pump and, later, a heart transplant. These same family members had also developed Type 2 diabetes as adults.

Obviously there is strong genetic component to their health issues, but I believe it goes much deeper, to the emotional attitudes held by each of them. We will explore these in great detail in Chapter 3; for now, suffice it to say the heart attacks gave me and my cousins a great deal to process with regard to our familial patterns.

Based on what I know about my granddaddy's life, he did not have it easy. His parents were emotionally unavailable, and his mother, my great-grandmother, had schizophrenia. Granddaddy went on to abuse his own children - physically with his sons, sexually with my mom and verbally with all of them. He was also a serial adulterer. My grandmother was clinically depressed and checked out of her life situation with pills and alcohol. She even tried to commit suicide when my mother was twelve.

As mentioned above, my uncle also died of a heart attack at age sixty-five. While speaking with his daughter I learned that she never got the emotional love and support from him, which has created relationship issues in her life. She revealed that her father constantly said that he would die at sixty-five. Was this something he manifested - a self-fulfilling prophecy - or did he intuit that this was when he would leave this world?

I also spoke with the daughter of the aunt who had survived the heart attack and subsequent transplant. My conversations with this cousin led me to explore what the heart problems are about in order to heal them in our generation. When she was visiting for winter holiday, I took her through a healing of our ancestral bloodline so we could get to the root issue. What we discovered was this lack of self-love goes back many generations, all the way back to the time of the Vikings. Our male ancestor came forth to show us his life of feeling unloved and unworthy, which was then passed down our genetic line. We went through a process to heal our ancestor and the rest of our lineage so that we can make the transition to self-love.

Armed with this knowledge, my cousins and I have an opportunity to examine our lives and our emotional attitudes to determine how much work there is to be done if we want to change the family health issues. My commitment is to live in a way that is all about self-love. This will enable me to give to my husband and children the love and emotional attention they want and need to thrive.

I don't know as much about my dad's side of the family. My grandmother died of ovarian cancer before I was born. My aunt believes it was self-manifested as a way to get away from my grandfather. I am not aware of anyone else on Dad's side of the family experiencing cancer. My grandfather lived a long and fairly healthy life. My dad had emergency open heart surgery when I was eighteen, narrowly avoiding a heart attack. The strained relationship between my dad and his sister, and his sister with their father, leads me to believe that life wasn't great in their household. There is anger and resentment running deep.

Exercise 2.2: Write Your Story About Your Ancestral Relationships

Think about the story of your grandparents and your great-grandparents. Write what you know in as much detail as you can. You may wish to do this here, write it in a journal or type it on your computer, whatever is best for you.

_____

_____

_____

_____

_____

_____

_____

_____

_____

_____

_____

_____

_____

_____

_____

_____

_____

_____

Love Relationships

Our love relationships commonly mirror the feelings and emotions we had growing up in our family. To help you understand this, I share my love story.

I was an early bloomer in my love life. My first boyfriend was in preschool, and I had my first kiss with him on the playground. My boy crazy thoughts continued throughout elementary school; indeed, I spent much of first and second grade chasing boys around the school playground and kissing them whenever possible.

In middle school, kissing boys turned into more. I had one boyfriend with whom I did a lot of exploring with at the movie theater and in his bedroom – these were my first second- and third- base make out sessions. I remember feeling intense butterflies. I could think about him and my stomach would churn. After we broke up, I continued my serial relation-ships through middle school.

In high school, my relationships turned more sexual in nature. Early in my freshman year, I started dating a senior. It was the first relationship I can remember being insecure in. Maybe it was his age. Maybe it was his best friend, a senior girl who didn't seem to like me much. He seemed to like me a lot, though, and I liked him right back. My birthday and Christmas were coming up and he talked about buying me a black pearl ring. I never did get the ring, but the day after my fifteenth birthday, I got a very different kind of birthday gift. He came over when my mom wasn't home. We were making out in the living room, which led to us having sex on my couch. That's how I lost my virginity.

The next day, he broke up with me, and a week later I found out he was dating a sophomore. I was heartbroken. I had given up my virginity to him because I thought I loved him and that he loved me. A few months later he tried to talk me into getting back together with me. I refused, as I knew I deserved better, and I didn't trust him. I had a few more boyfriends during my freshman year and the following summer before I met my next learning experience.

The fall of my sophomore year, I met a cute guy. We went out on our first date and ended up back at his house. We went to his room, where he date raped me. Because I had been sexual with a couple other guys, I was confused about the situation. I was angry, but I kept dating him because I did not want him to spread rumors about us having sex on the first date. I learned that saying no doesn't work.

After our breakup I moved on quickly; in fact, I would have one boyfriend after another throughout the rest of high school, college and graduate school. In college, I had two serious boyfriends, each lasting a year. The first one was inexperienced at relationships as I was his first girlfriend; the second ended up dating one of my best friends after we broke up. Around the time I graduated college, I started dating an older man who decided to move to Chicago with me. I broke up with him shortly after we arrived. Although he was emotionally available and lovely, I was damaged and unable to accept his love.

For the remainder of graduate school I had a series of relationships, both long distance and local, with the guys who were emotionally unavailable. I perpetuated my pattern of feeling sad and abandoned. This continued through my two marriages.

While on my first date with husband number one, I had a vivid memory of a past life we had shared (he actually had the same vision at the same time when we were looking into each other's eyes). We were in Scotland during the time of William Wallace (Braveheart). We were new in our relationship when he went off to war to fight with William. He never came back to me. Because our relationship ended abruptly in that life, I felt we had unfinished business in this one. That contributed to my feeling the need to have the relationship with him, even when things started getting bad.

Exercise 2.3: Write Your Story About Your Love Relationships

Think about all of the significant relationships you have had throughout your life, specifically love relationships. Write what you can remember in as much detail as you can. You may wish to do this here, write it in a journal or type it on your computer, whatever is best for you.

_____

_____

_____

_____

_____

_____

_____

_____

_____

_____

_____

_____

_____

_____

_____

_____

_____

_____

_____

Timeline of Events – Relationships and Health Issues

Now that you have written out your stories of your relationships with your parents, ancestors and significant others, you will use some of the information for the next exercise.

Exercise 2.4: Timeline Exercise

For this exercise, you will need a large piece of paper or poster board and colored pencils or markers. Create a timeline for yourself of your love relationships in one color. Using a second color, focus on your immediate family on the timeline. Include any significant events in your life, such as your parents divorcing, parents remarrying, death or loss of a parent, first kiss, losing your virginity, marriage, divorce, etc.

Using a third color, indicate any significant health issues or illnesses you had on the timeline. With a fourth color, indicate any specific negative emotions you remember having at different points in your life.

A chronological timeline for this particular exercise is best, for it will allow you to see recurring patterns clearly. You do not need to draw a straight line; instead, you may wish to use a curved line, oscillating line or a spiral to fit everything onto one piece of paper. You can draw stacks of lines for each decade you have lived. Be as thorough as possible, including all the facts you can recall.

Once you have all of the information documented on your timeline, begin looking for patterns in your relationships and health issues. You may discover patterns of abandonment, abuse, power, putting other people's needs above your own, or other negative experiences. You may also notice certain times in your life where you had positive relationships and experiences. Circle any areas on your timeline where there are recurring patterns and make notes on what was going on at the time.

By writing your personal stories about your relationships and then mapping them onto a timeline, you will start to open up the memories and discover deeply rooted issues you were not even aware of – issues you can now begin to heal. The deeper you go into exploring the roots of your relationships with your family and loved ones, the more extra-ordinary the healing will be.

"And in the end, the love you take is equal to the love you make."
— Paul McCartney

3

Revealing Your Blocks and Limitations

"Your task is not to seek for love,
but merely to seek and find all
the barriers within yourself that you
have built against it."
— Rumi

*I*n the last chapter, you mapped out your relationship and health history on a timeline. This exercise is an important first step in having you think about your relationship patterns, belief systems and overall health. You will now be using the information to go even deeper. If you have not created a timeline, please review Chapter 2 and complete the timeline exercise before beginning the upcoming exercises.

To get the most out of the process of revealing your blockages, limitations and wounds, I want you to set aside specific time to complete these exercises. Be as detailed as you can in answering the questions.

If emotions come up as you are thinking about your life, use that to dig even deeper. If you experience pain or discomfort, remember that emotions are not who you are, they are just the body's way of expressing stored energy. Feel them and then let them pass. If you uncover a major trauma you have a hard time dealing with on your own, I strongly recommend talking to a professional counselor who can help you deal with it.

This chapter is broken down into two major sections. In the first section, you will assess your life, health, personal values, faults and virtues, and beliefs, both positive and negative. In the second section, you will assess your past relationship(s) and your ideal relationship and how those relate to you.

Assessing Yourself and Your Life

In the next set of exercises, you will have the opportunity to assess and analyze your current life and love reality and compare that to where you want to be. This will give you a starting point from which you can map out a new direction.

What areas of your life are working for you? What areas are not working? This is not about judgment, but about identifying a problem in order to fix it. You may think your issue is in one area or another, only to find it originates somewhere else entirely. It is important that you are completely honest with yourself when answering the questions. The deeper you are able to go, the more you will get out of these exercises.

Exercise 3.1: Life Questions

Answer the following questions below.

1. How would I rate my life – on a scale from 1-10 (1 = poor; 10 = excellent):

      Mentally: _____

      Emotionally: _____

      Physically: _____

      Spiritually: _____

Comments:

_____

_____

_____

_____

_____

2. What is my life's purpose?

_____

_____

_____

_____

_____

3. Is there another life purpose I would rather be living?

_____

_____

_____

_____

_____

4. What are my passions in life?

_____

_____

_____

_____

_____

5. What brings me joy?

_____

_____

_____

_____

_____

6. What do I need to forgive myself/others for?

_____

_____

_____

_____

_____

7. What do I want in my life moving forward?

_____

_____

_____

_____

_____

8. What is really important to me in terms of love?

_____

_____

_____

_____

_____

9. What are my love goals?

_____

_____

_____

_____

_____

10. How do I currently view love?

_____

_____

_____

_____

_____

Personal Health Issues

Our body is an amazing vehicle that visibly and viscerally demonstrates our underlying unhealthy and negative thoughts and emotional issues. It expresses these thoughts by way of illness and pain showing up in our bodies. Oftentimes, we are unaware of the thoughts in our subconscious mind. When we have health problems, we can uncover the emotional root cause of the issue, which allows us the opportunity to heal it.

Many of us had illnesses in childhood that did not carry through to adulthood. We may have illnesses and ailments as adults that we did not have as children. It is important to examine our complete health history to understand how our bodies express our underlying emotions. We can determine if childhood beliefs have continued into adulthood, as demonstrated through an illness that evolves to become more chronic or extreme. Or perhaps you have already healed an emotion as an adult and the ailment went away.

To understand the emotional causes of illness in the body, I reference two main books: *You Can Heal Your Life* by Louise Hay and *The Secret Language of Your Body* by Inna Segal. I particularly appreciate *The Secret Language of Your Body*, as it goes into more detail about each illness. It also has exercises to help you release the illness.

For you to understand what this health examination looks like and how it translates into emotional issues, I will share with you a brief portion of my health story. You will have the opportunity to examine your personal health history and the emotional meanings in this section.

My Personal Health History

As mentioned earlier, while growing up, I experienced childhood trauma which led to different health issues throughout my life. From birth until the age of two, I had constant earaches. The doctors put tubes in my ears, which alleviated the majority of the earaches, though I continued to have random ear problems throughout the rest of my childhood, as well as several bouts of tonsillitis.

When I was six, I began suffering from asthma attacks. My doctors couldn't figure out what was triggering them, so their solution was to give me an inhaler. The true cause - an allergy to milk and corn – wasn't discovered until I went to a naturopath at the age of sixteen. When I was twenty-eight, I went to a healer who helped me discover and heal the root cause of the asthma. It was an emotional reaction to my dad's neglect and my feelings of being unworthy and abandoned. Since acknowledging and healing the emotion, I have not experienced the allergy asthma.

I also had skin issues for much of my life. As a child I developed an allergic reaction to the sun and grass and would occasionally break out in rashes when I had too much exposure. When in graduate school, I had a serious outbreak of guttate psoriasis, the rarest form and one doctors knew next to nothing about. The flaky red patches covered my body from head to toe, making me feel miserable and gross. After trying several topical treatments, the doctor had me do light therapy, which made it go away. Strep throat is a known trigger for guttate psoriasis, but in my case the root cause was stress and anxiety. That particular time was the most stressful of my life to that point. To this day, when I get too stressed my psoriasis comes back in random patches.

Symptoms and Emotional Meaning
(from *The Secret Language of Your Body* – Inna Segal):

Earaches – Feeling judged and judging others. Not listening to your own insight and wisdom. Not wanting to hear what is being said, trying to block other people out. Feeling like others want to control you. Blame, frustration, anger, misunderstanding, arguments. Refusing to change your mind or perspective. Feeling ignored, unnoticed, resentful, unsteady.

Tonsillitis – Feeling defensive, controlling, fearful. Believing what you have to express is not important and others will not want to hear it. Suppressing your creativity and joy. Underestimating your talents and abilities. Clinginess. Seeking others' permission and support for what you do.

Asthma – Trying too hard to please others. Wanting to be perfect. Difficulty saying no, standing up for yourself, and expressing how you feel. Pushing yourself to the limit until you feel exhausted and out of breath. Feeling weak, anxious, and disempowered. Allowing others to control you. Feeling hurt, stuck, caged.

Allergies – Feeling annoyed and aggravated by other people. Giving away your power. Blaming people and events for your negative reactions. Obsession with people who have hurt you. Difficulty forgiving and seeing the blessing in this hurt. Allowing yourself to be controlled or manipulated by others, and then punishing them by withholding love and kindness. Not knowing how to create boundaries with others.

Food Allergies – Feeling irritated by what is happening around you. Extremely sensitive to other people's behaviors and beliefs about you. Feeling frustrated that your discomforts with life have not been heard and solved. Resisting life. Too focused on what you like and don't like. Not allowing full expression of who you are.

Psoriasis – Insecure, rejected, irritated. Needing to find someone to blame rather than taking responsibility. Suppressing feelings until they erupt in anger. Carrying deep disappointments. Self-hatred and self-punishment. Feeling lost, like you don't know where you belong.

Rash – Oversensitive, insecure, fearful. Self-imposed limitations that irritate or do not serve you. Small explosions of anger erupting on your skin. Feeling threatened by someone or something. Suppressed emotions that can no longer be pushed down.

When I look at the underlying meanings of the significant ailments I had growing up and even into my early adulthood, it is no surprise that I developed the ailments I did. My body was expressing the emotions I couldn't express for myself.

As you read through the symptoms of your ailments and their underlying emotional causes, you may find that these causes resonate fully or just in part. Trust your intuition about what is true for you and your situation. Take the parts that make sense and leave the rest. Go as deep into your understanding as you can to get the most out of this exercise.

Exercise 3.2: Make a list of your recurring health issues as a child and as an adult.

This can be a diagnosed illness or physical aches and pains. Research the underlying emotional issue for each ailment and write those down. Indicate if the health issue is past or current. This exercise will help you to become aware of deep emotional issues you may not be aware of yet. I recommend getting the two books I mentioned, but if that isn't possible, you can begin with an internet search.

Your Health Issues	*Underlying Emotional Issue*	*Past or Current*

Family Health Issues

Everyone's parents and extended family have health issues which may or may not be expressed in their own bodies. Therefore, it is important to explore the underlying emotional issues prevalent in your family, as it will reveal potential patterns of belief systems and emotions running through the ancestral bloodline. When you know the issues, you can determine if you have some of them hidden deep inside yourself, and, if so, heal them before they become major health problems that are more challenging to reverse when fully expressed in the body. This will help to stop the illnesses propagating in future generations as well.

As you investigate your family lineage, keep in mind that your relatives' health issues are not predestined to become your own. We all have the power to change our emotional and physical environments, thereby preventing and healing dis-ease. For more information on this, I highly recommend reading *The Biology of Belief* by Dr. Bruce Lipton; *You are the Placebo: Making Your Mind Matter* by Dr. Joe Dispenza; and *The Spontaneous Healing of Belief: Shattering the Paradigm of False Limits* by Gregg Braden.

Let's return for a moment to the ancestral illnesses on my mother's side of the family. My grandfather, my mother, my uncle and my aunt all had heart attacks at age sixty-five. For my grandfather and uncle, those attacks were fatal; my mom and aunt survived, but Mom continues to struggle with strokes and other heart/circulation issues and my aunt is now recovering from a heart transplant.

There are two issues going on here. First, there is likely a strong genetic component to heart disease on this side of my family. Second, there is something about the age of sixty-five that is significant. I will only focus on the underlying emotional side of heart issues here, and in doing so I borrow from *The Secret Language of Your Body* by Inna Segal:

Heart problems: Feeling blocked, unenthusiastic, uninspired, flat, depressed, heavy-hearted, stressed. Thinking life is too hard and you can't be bothered with dealing with it. Feeling close-hearted, wounded, rejected, hardened, cold. Giving up on love, not believing you deserve it. Frequent self-criticism and self-deprecation. Feeling worthless, angry and bitter. Waiting until things come to a boil to let your feelings out. Taking on too much responsibility, then feeling stressed and anxious. Giving too much of yourself and pushing further than you can handle. Not listening to your heart. Feeling unfulfilled, disappointed, put-down and lonely. Holding on to a deep-seated fear of being hurt or having your heart broken.

Heart attack: Stubbornness, stress, inflexibility, obnoxious attitude, a "my way or the highway" approach. Selfish, ignorant, controlling. Too focused on money, achievement, and winning. Neglect of your health and family. Suppression, envy, hardness. Needing to be right. Feeling unloved, easily hurt, holding on to guilt and regret. Thinking that you know everything – that you don't need anyone's help or advice.

Stroke: Feeling useless, hopeless, inadequate. Overwhelming pressure and stress. Unable to handle the situation you are in. Giving up. Feeling like a failure. Shutting down. Refusing to change and failing to understand why what you have done did not work.

The heart is in the fourth seal or chakra of the body, which represents love. It makes sense, then, that a lack of self-love is an underlying emotional cause of heart problems. In the case of my family, this lack of love, combined with anger and resentment, created the environment able to express a genetic predisposition of the illness. Currently, my cousins and I do not have any heart issues we are aware of. However, if we continue to live the way we were raised, it is likely that one or more of us will experience heart problems in the future.

Another illness that runs through my mother's side of the family is Type 2 Diabetes, which, as mentioned earlier, has been experienced by the same relatives with heart issues. Inna Segal also describes the underlying emotional causes of this disease in *The Secret Language of Your Body*.

Type 2 Diabetes: Fear of fully participating in life. Great need for control and to know things. Deep need for attention and approval. A constant craving for love paired with a belief that you are unworthy and undeserving. Deep-seated guilt. Belief that you have to struggle to survive. Often losing yourself in relationships. Constant need for sweetness to mask feelings of weakness, limitation, and the belief that there is not enough. Stuck in your own world of limitation and lack.

From a medical perspective, Type 2 Diabetes is developed in adulthood and believed to form from poor diet and lack of exercise. My understanding is that chronic emotions of lack of self-love and worthiness are often expressed by eating poorly and not taking care of the body, thus leading to the expressed illness of diabetes as an adult.

Type 1 Diabetes develops in childhood and is not correlated to diet in the same way. It's underlying emotional causes, however, are very similar to Type 2.

Type 1 Diabetes: Needing sweetness, attention, love and care. Feeling insecure, unsure of yourself, overly needy, and reliant on others. Self-centered and focused on your inadequacies. Wanting to appear indispensable to others. Listening to and surrounding yourself with too much negativity.

Neither I nor my cousins currently express diabetes, but growing up, I had major bouts of hypoglycemia (low blood sugar). It was something I could regulate with the types of food and how often I ate. Hypoglycemia has the same emotional meanings as diabetes. Knowing my emotional wounds as a child, I can clearly see the correlation and how accurate the meaning is for me.

The following exercise will help you to become aware of deep emotional issues that run in your family.

Exercise 3.3: Make a list of health issues occurring in your immediate family, as well as those which may occur in your extended blood-related family (i.e. aunts, uncles, and grandparents). Research the underlying emotional issue for each ailment and write them down. Indicate who in your family has the issue. If the health issue occurs in two or more related family members, you may wish to explore further for yourself, as it could have a higher chance of being expressed in your body unless you actively address it.

Health Issues	Underlying Emotional Issue	Family Member(s)

Personal Values

Values are a person's principles or standards of behavior or one's judgment of what is important in life. Each person has a different set of values depending on how they grew up and how they interpret the experiences in their life. We place different levels of importance on values, some being highly important, others less so. Sometimes we may think a value is important to us, but upon examining find that our behavior is not in alignment with that value.

Some examples of personal values include: love, family, health, truth, honesty, integrity, loyalty, commitment, creativity, positivity, dependability, open-mindedness, innovation, reliability, compassion, optimism, respect, courage, passion, perseverance, discipline, accountability, diligence, service to others, education, motivation, spirit of adventure, efficiency, consistency, innovation, humor, cooperation, courtesy, dedication, patriotism, environmentalism.

Exercise 3.4: Think about your personal values. List them below and rank them in order of importance. Indicate values consistent with your life, leaving those that aren't consistent unmarked.

Once you have completed the table, take a look at the values you said were important and those that your behavior is not currently in alignment with. If the values unmarked are truly important to you, you now have an opportunity to see how you can better incorporate these values into your life in a more consistent way. You may determine some values are not important. This exercise is all about uncovering your authentic self and living in accordance with who you truly are, not who you or others think you should be.

Personal Values	*Rank in order of Importance*	*Values consistent in your life*

Faults & Virtues

We are our own worst critics, judging ourselves harshly and comparing ourselves to others, which contributes to our unhappiness and lack of wellbeing. When we are able to see our faults and make shifts to understand the positive virtues of those faults, we can re-wire our brain to reduce and eliminate the negative self-talk.

A fault is defined as an unattractive or unsatisfactory feature, especially in a person's character. It can be thought of as a character flaw. An example of a "fault" I have is impatience.

A virtue is defined as a behavior showing high moral standards. If we flip the "fault" of impatience to seeing it as a virtue, we might consider someone with this quality as a go-getter, a force of nature who makes things happen.

Exercise 3.5: Make a list of your faults/flaws. These might be things you see in yourself or things you have been criticized by others for. Even if you don't agree with other peoples' assessment of your flaws, list them anyway. Next to each one, write how it can be viewed in a positive light.

Your Personal Faults	*Positive Virtues of Faults*

Negative vs. Positive Beliefs

Belief systems can form from birth, or even in the womb, passed down through the family bloodline and the environment. These beliefs are indirect and not really ours to keep. Our beliefs can also be formed throughout life as we live through various experiences. The meanings we assign to those experiences become our beliefs, both negative and positive.

It's important to assess what we believe about ourselves and the world we live in, and to understand from where those beliefs came. We can then determine if we want to carry those beliefs forward. We can release old baggage that doesn't serve us anymore. We can cultivate healthy beliefs that support and nurture us.

Negative Beliefs

Exercise 3.6: Make a list of your negative beliefs. Next to each one, indicate when you formed this belief and if you believe it to be true in your life.

Negative Belief	When Belief was formed	Is it true?

Positive Beliefs

Exercise 3.7: Make a list of your positive beliefs. Next to each one, indicate when you formed this belief and if you know it to be true in your life.

Positive Belief	When Belief was formed	Is it true?

Assessment of Love Relationships – Past, Present, Future

The previous exercises were all about you and your specific issues and belief systems. Now we are going to turn our attention to how we view the partners in our relationships, past, present and future.

The people in our lives often act as mirrors of who and what we are. When we see something we like in someone, it is usually because we recognize a similar favorable quality within ourselves. When we see and judge something we don't like, we need to take a deep look to see where we might possess that quality we don't appreciate. We have to be truthful with ourselves if we are going to truly heal our wounds.

One of the best mirrors we can look to for evidence of these qualities is our current and most recent significant others. If you are currently in a long-term relationship, your partner is the one you will be using for the next exercise. If you are currently single, your most recent long-term partner will be used for this exercise. If you have only been dating your partner for a short while, it is a good idea to do the exercise for the current new partner, as well as your last significant partner.

My Past Relationship Assessment

I went through this process while divorcing my second husband, so he served as my mirror. Once I had listed his negative qualities, I then had to determine whether I too possessed each quality. I had to be honest with myself. Was the quality there all the time, or did it only come out in certain circumstances or with certain people? With most of the qualities I deemed negative, I was able to identify specific situations in my life where that quality was true for me.

There were a few qualities I noted in my ex that I did not feel I possessed. These were immaturity, one-upping, and being close-minded. I consider myself to be mature and open-minded, with no need to be better than anyone else. That said, these were far outweighed by the list of negative qualities I observed in both my ex and myself.

Once I had completed this assessment, I then had to decide whether I was willing to change all of the negative qualities. The answer was yes, so I became conscious of where I was expressing the qualities and actively modified my behavior and thoughts in those situations. I had to retrain and rewire my brain patterns.

The following exercises will help you to identify areas in your life you may want to work on for the purpose of finding self-love and happiness. Be patient with yourself. Becoming consciously aware of our thoughts and actions can be more challenging than it sounds and is an ongoing practice.

Assessment of Past Relationship(s)

Exercise 3.8: Think about your last significant relationship (or current relationship, if applicable), and fill in the table below. (You may want to do this list for your previous two relationships as well.)

Characteristic disliked in last partner	Where in your life do you possess those characteristics (if at all)?	In areas you don't possess the characteristic, is it the opposite or a reflection?	Areas you are unwilling to change

Assessment of the Ideal Relationship

No matter what relationship situation you are currently in, there is value in describing your perfect, ideal partner. This lets you observe how close or how far away you are from having the qualities you want in your dream relationship.

My Ideal Partner Assessment

I created a list of the characteristics I wanted my perfect mate to possess. My list was much longer than the negative qualities of my ex (and myself) that I had created. Once the characteristics were listed, I determined which of those characteristics I was not matched to yet. In my case, I was not matched to being patient, fun/playful, funny/witty and easy-going.

According to the Law of Attraction and quantum mechanics, we can only attract what we are aligned with completely. I couldn't attract a partner that was patient if I was not patient myself. This was a crucial piece of the puzzle and yet another thing I had to become consciously aware of while rewiring my brain.

Whether you are currently in a relationship or single, this next exercise will reveal to you the areas you will want to address for creating a healthy loving relationship with your ideal partner (and yourself).

As you go through this process, you will find that some of the characteristics are easier to transform than others. Learning to be patient was one of my biggest challenges. I experienced an amazing lesson in patience when I found my perfect mate, which I'll talk about more in Chapter 7.

Exercise 3.9: Think about yourself and your new ideal relationship and fill in the table below:

Your personal positive characteristics	*Your perfect mate's characteristics*	*Areas not matched yet*

Now that you have completed these exercises, you have uncovered qualities and beliefs which may not be serving you and the greater good of your life. It is up to you to decide whether or not you want to address your underlying emotions and behaviors to heal those parts of yourself that are hurt and blocked.

Final thought: Be honest with yourself about your inner beliefs and thought patterns. We must reveal to heal. In the space below, take time to journal about your realizations and the themes and patterns you want to change. In the next chapter, I guide you through exercises, journeys and methods to help you heal your blocks and limitations.

"People think a soul mate is your perfect fit, and that's what everyone wants. But a true soul mate is a mirror, the person who shows you everything that is holding you back, the person who brings you to your own attention so you can change your life.

A true soul mate is probably the most important person you'll ever meet, because they tear down your walls and smack you awake. But to live with a soul mate forever? Nah. Too painful. Soul mates, they come into your life just to reveal another layer of yourself to you, and then leave.

A soul mate's purpose is to shake you up, tear apart your ego a little bit, show you your obstacles and addictions, break your heart open so new light can get in, make you so desperate and out of control that you have to transform your life, then introduce you to your spiritual master..."
— Elizabeth Gilbert, *Eat, Pray, Love*

4

Healing and Releasing Old Blocks

"Love yourself first and everything else falls into line.
You really have to love yourself to get anything
done in this world."
— Lucille Ball

*Y*ou have exposed the blockages, limitations and old wounds keeping you from creating a beautiful life that you love. Now it is time to release and heal those injuries and belief systems. It is time to rewire your brain and create new patterns of thoughts and emotions. It is time to become a whole, healthy person filled with self-love.

After leaving my second husband, I decided I did not want to continue making the same relationship mistakes I had made for the majority of my life. To do so, I had to embark on a journey to find self-love, so that I would be okay with myself even if I was never in another intimate relationship. In this chapter, I will walk you through different exercises, methods and journeys I personally experienced to heal myself and rediscover who I am at my core.

I encourage you to use the space provided in this workbook to complete the exercises. You may also wish to use a separate journal for the lengthier writing pieces. I want you to get the most out of this, so please complete as many of the exercises and experiences as you can. Trust me, it will be worth it!

That said, you are a unique individual with your own personal blocks, so do not feel pressured to do them all. Start with the ones that resonate with you. After completing those you can choose to do more. Everyone has a different journey to take. For some, the healing process can take weeks, months or years. For others, it may only take moments.

Healing Exercises

Exercise 4.1 - Write a Sacred Soul Love Contract

In the space below, on a separate sheet of paper or in a journal, create and sign a contract for yourself clearly stating your intention for loving yourself for the next month. It can be as general or specific as you want. Be honest and realistic with yourself about what you are willing to commit to, then review it throughout the month to remind yourself of that commitment.

_____

_____

_____

_____

_____

_____

_____

_____

_____

_____

_____

_____

_____

_____

_____

_____

_____

_____

_____

Exercise 4.2 - Write Commitments to Yourself

Make a list of the commitments you are willing to make to yourself moving forward.

As an example, I have provided a list of the commitments I made to myself. I printed out that list and still look at it every so often to remind myself when I get off track.

- I am enough for myself.
- I honor and cherish myself.
- I value and respect myself.
- I take full responsibility for the circumstances of my life.
- I continue to learn and grow in self-awareness.
- I am honest and authentic in all of my interactions with myself and others.
- I live in abundance.
- I live in joy.
- I am the source of my happiness, love, approval and safety.
- I live in gratitude.
- I am an excellent giver and receiver.
- I take care of my mind, body and soul.
- I am patient and gentle with myself.
- I love myself unconditionally at every age, size, shape and life experience.

Commitments to Myself:

_____

_____

_____

_____

_____

_____

_____

_____

_____

_____

_____

_____

_____

_____

_____

_____

_____

_____

_____

_____

_____

_____

_____

_____

_____

_____

_____

_____

Exercise 4.3 - Write a Sacred Soul Love Mission Statement

Create a Sacred Soul Love Mission Statement. Take time to write a mission statement, specifically for having love in your life. Think about what you want to have in a relationship and include that as part of your statement.

The purpose of my love life is. . .

_____

_____

_____

_____

_____

_____

_____

_____

_____

_____

_____

_____

_____

_____

_____

_____

_____

_____

_____

_____

_____

_____

_____

_____

Exercise 4.4 – Letter to Your Future Self

On a separate sheet of paper, write a letter to yourself from yourself, one year in the future. Tell yourself about all of the wonderful things that happened during the year and where you are now in your life. Include as many details as possible to make it even more real.

Exercise 4.5 – Your Story, Five Years in the Future

On a separate sheet of paper or in a journal, write a story about your life five years in the future, as if it is already happening. Include as much detail and description as you can. Include where you live, what kind of profession you are in (or retirement), your relationship status, etc. Include the feelings and emotions you have in your future life.

_____

_____

_____

_____

_____

_____

_____

_____

_____

_____

_____

_____

_____

_____

_____

_____

_____

_____

_____

_____

_____

_____

_____

Exercise 4.6 - Self-Care Activities

Make a list below of all of the self-care activities you can do for yourself that you enjoy or want to try out. This can include getting a facial, massage, doing yoga and so on. Include any other activities that sound fun and might require more planning. Maybe you've always wanted to try skydiving or downhill skiing or take a cooking class. After you have made this list, you can refer back to it when you are planning your day, week or month.

_____   _____

_____   _____

_____   _____

_____   _____

_____   _____

_____   _____

_____   _____

_____   _____

_____   _____

_____   _____

_____   _____

_____   _____

_____   _____

_____   _____

_____   _____

_____   _____

_____   _____

_____   _____

_____   _____

Exercise 4.7 - Burning Words Exercise

On a separate sheet of paper, make a list of all of the things you want to release in your life. Once you have your list, burn the paper in a safe space, watching the words turn to ashes, mutating the energy. After the paper is burned, take a piece of food or a drink you love and consciously imbue it with new qualities you want to take into your body. As you chew the food or drink the liquid, feel those new qualities permeating every cell in your body.

Exercise 4.8 - Mirror Work

Below are two very different exercises using a mirror. These mirror work exercises are a bit different from the mirror work taught by Louise Hay. You may wish to incorporate her work as well.

Mirror 1 - Stand or sit in front of a mirror, whatever is most comfortable for you, so long as you are able to see your face. Look deeply into your eyes, which are the windows to the soul. Continue to do so for at least five minutes. Infuse love into your reflection. See the beauty in who you truly are, not just the exterior body. If you notice your mind start to drift to negative thoughts, quickly shift your thoughts to love to get yourself back on track. Do this every day for at least thirty days.

Mirror 2 – Sit in front of a mirror in a dark room, with only a lit candle next to the mirror to light your face. With meditative music on, look into your eyes in the mirror. Allow your mind to relax, blinking as little as possible. Keep staring into your eyes. When you are relaxed enough, the mirror will turn black for a moment as you move into your subconscious mind. Don't be afraid. You are safe. You may start to see your face change shape, form and color. You may see scenes in the mirror. Just observe what you see without judgment. You are tapping into your past lives. Know that you are not your body in this life. You are a soul that has lived many lives. I recommend doing this exercise for at least thirty minutes to give yourself enough time to relax into the process.

Exercise 4.9 - Self-talk/behavior - See it, Stop it, Flip it

See it, Stop it, Flip it is a powerful method that repatterns negative thoughts and behaviors. It helps you to become more conscious of your patterns and triggers so you can actively change them. When you notice a particular thought or behavior in yourself, see it in that moment; this will help you to stop it. When you stop it in your mind, make a small physical movement to go with your conscious thought of "Stop." The movement can be whatever you choose and as discreet as you need it to be. Once you stop it, you then flip it to a new thought or behavior you want to create as the new pattern. Use a different physical movement with each new thought. The physical movement paired with the thought helps to anchor it in the body and the brain. The more conscious you are about your thoughts and behaviors, the quicker you will be able to shift your mindset.

When I went through this process, I told a few people close to me, and who I completely trusted, what I was doing. I asked them to help me notice any particular thoughts and behaviors they saw and (nicely) call me out. It can be difficult to be aware of our actions in every moment, and our ego often gets in the way of what our higher self might want.

A similar exercise that helps rewire the brain is wearing a rubber bracelet that can be snapped when you notice negative thoughts. When you snap the bracelet, it gets you out of your head so you can shift your thoughts.

Alternative Healing Methods

During my healing, I tapped into my resources for help, including several different types of energy healers. These healers opened and balanced my chakras, thereby moving and releasing stuck energy. They also helped me to identify blockages using applied kinesiology (muscle testing) and then used a variety of tools, including EFT tapping, to neutralize my emotions regarding my relationships with my father and ex-husbands.

I used Past Life Regression Therapy to get to the root cause of some of my issues and shift them at the quantum level, thereby changing my past, present and future. I loved the Past Life Regression Therapy so much I studied with world-renowned past life expert, Denise Linn, to become a practitioner.

Quantum mechanics says there is no past or future, there is only the now. The mind does not know the difference between what we are experiencing when our eyes are open and when they are closed; this means we can go to a particular time in our life and change the story in a dramatic way. Alternatively, we can change the meaning of the story to change the trajectory of a lifetime. The changes propagate through the rest of the timelines to rewire the brain and the overall memory and experience of the event or situation. These changes become apparent in the weeks and months following a Past Life Regression session.

Health & Exercise

As part of the healing process, it is imperative to treat your body well. This includes eating nutritious, healthy foods and getting regular exercise. If you are conscious about what you are putting into your body and the emotions you are feeling as you eat and drink, you will become aware of what is supporting you and not supporting you in terms of your health. You may find some foods don't agree with the new you that you are working to create.

Exercise does not have to be intense. Moving your body for half an hour, three to five times a week, is the general recommendation and sufficient, unless you want to dramatically change the way your body looks. My advice is do what feels good to your soul. Don't use working out to fill a void of unworthiness. You are beautiful and loveable at any size and shape. Moving your body keeps your bones and muscles healthy. Try not to focus on the number on the scale.

Self-dating and Activities with Friends

It is important in this process that you find joy and fun in your life before you bring a new partner into your world. If you have recently left a relationship, it may take some time to rediscover who you are and what you enjoy, and to create a life you love living.

Make room in your schedule for dating, self-care and relaxation. If you are too busy to spend time with yourself and with friends, then you will be too busy to date your perfect partner. Like clutter clearing from a physical space, you need to clutter clear your schedule. Eliminate nonessential aspects of your schedule so you can make time to have fun. This is critical to your success.

Take yourself out on dates. Don't be afraid to try new things so you can see what interests you have and what you don't like. When you go out, treat yourself like you would want your perfect mate to treat you. Wine and dine yourself. Woo yourself. Be your own best friend.

Do fun activities outside your house with one or more friends. Explore your town and area. Meet new people. Get outside of boring routines and expand your horizons.

At the same time I was actively assessing myself, I was also dating myself. The idea behind this was to figure out what activities I enjoyed and what I did not enjoy. I was to treat myself like I would want my date to treat me. I had to give myself the same kind of love and attention I would want a mate to give me. It turns out that I'm really good at doing things on my own. I knew that from all the solo traveling I had done while in graduate school, but it was good to be reminded that I enjoy my own company.

For me, this meant taking myself out to nice restaurants and watching movies at the theater and at home. I could eat where I wanted. I could watch what I wanted. It also meant taking long baths and treating myself nicely.

I was able to go out with my girlfriends whenever I wanted as well. I did not have to ask permission. After my second divorce, I took a trip with a few friends to Cancun, Mexico, which was a good first step in my freedom. At the end of that trip, I took a day to leave my friends and do what I wanted to do, which was swim with dolphins and explore Isla Mujeres. They stayed behind to sit and drink in the pool all day. I wanted to explore, so I did. I felt free and happy.

> *"You're always with yourself, so you might as well enjoy the company."*
> **— Diane Von Furstenberg**

Travel Solo

Traveling by yourself is a freeing experience. You get to decide what you do and where you go at all times of the day and night. You can travel a short distance just for the weekend or you can plan a much longer trip abroad. Whatever you decide, give yourself space to fully be with yourself.

If you have never been on a solo trip, you may feel some fear around your safety, particularly if you are traveling to a strange locale. Make sure you travel to a place with some comfort features that will also allow you to step outside your comfort zone. This could mean going to a country where people speak the same language as you or hiring a tour guide who can take you around and translate for you. You could book a trip through a travel agent with pre-planned activities where they pick you up at your hotel and drop you back off. You could join a tour that has every activity already planned out for you as well. Do what feels right for you, but be willing to step through your fear and grow.

For me, the highlight of this process was a two-week trip to Australia without friends or family. A lot of people told me how brave I was and that they could never do something like this. For me, there was no fear. I enjoyed the freedom of making the decisions and doing what I wanted in the moment. The trip was crafted to be a magical dream vacation, and it was perfect. It helped me fully re-establish myself as a sovereign being.

On the trip, I had a mixture of pre-planned activities, arranged by my travel agent, that I knew I would enjoy. I also had a set itinerary so I always knew someone would be picking me up and dropping me off at the various locations I was visiting. It took the worry out of the trip. I also allowed for some downtime so I could explore each place and be spontaneous.

"A healthy self-love means we have no compulsion to justify to ourselves or others why we take vacations, why we sleep late, why we buy new shoes, why we spoil ourselves from time to time. We feel comfortable doing things which add quality and beauty to life."
– Andrew Matthews

Additional Self-Support

Some of the methods I described above may not be enough for you, or you may want some additional traditional support in healing yourself. Before I started using the energy healing and similar modalities, I spent time in Al-Anon and in counseling.

Al-Anon, a twelve-step program for friends and family of alcoholics, was recommended to me by the court when I was divorcing my first husband. In the two years I attended meetings, I found a support system of people who completely understood what I had been through and were there to hold space for me to express my emotions in a way I had never been able to do. It was in these meetings that I was first able to start speaking about what I had been through with my husband and the abuse I had experienced. I learned what codependency was and realized that I had been codependent in the majority of my relationships while growing up. It was my way of trying to be loved. (If codependency is one of your issues, I highly recommend reading *Codependent No More: How to Stop Controlling Others and Start Caring for Yourself* by Melody Beattie.)

As mentioned earlier, I also spent nearly two years in couple's counseling before marrying my second husband. We had just had a baby and we were not getting along. I felt stuck. We did not communicate well with each other and there were a lot of hard times. My partner made enough changes in those two years that I decided to marry him when he asked a few months after our therapy ended. I still had doubts, but I had a support system with our therapist if we needed it.

Over time, my husband reverted back to some of the behaviors I didn't like, and we ended up in therapy one more time before I decided to leave him for good. Our issues were too big, and I was not willing to settle for a mediocre relationship.

Finding a counselor/therapist you can really trust is critical if you choose to go this path. They have different styles and ideologies, so finding someone who can help you with your particular issues is key to helping you heal.

Meditative Journeys of Healing

The following meditations are meant to help you heal some of the issues you exposed earlier in the workbook. The Past Life Regression and Ancestral Healing meditations are meant to focus on one issue at a time, as each blockage has a different root cause or experience. You can repeat these as many times as you want to heal different parts of yourself. The Journey to the Future meditation is to help you reveal any future issues that might not be apparent to you at this moment. Once you become aware of an issue, you can then heal it in this process as well.

I have these meditation recordings on the book website at www.MysticManta.com, so you can access them as needed. Alternatively, you can record yourself speaking these meditations to play back to yourself.

You want to do these mediations in a place where you can fully relax your body and mind without any distractions. The more relaxed you are, the easier it will be to access the subconscious mind and allow the changes to occur.

Past Life Regression Meditation

Get yourself into a comfortable, relaxed position. Close your eyes and take several deep breaths, allowing your mind and body to relax. Melt into the surface below you. Allow yourself to go deeper and deeper into your subconscious mind. You are safe. You are secure. All is well. Become one with your breath. Become one with your surroundings. Imagine a luminous white streaming light above your head. Open up your crown chakra and let the light flow through your body like a waterfall. As the white light flows through every part of your body, it is removing all blocked energy, stuck energy. The white light flows like a river down through your head and out the bottom of your feet, relaxing every part of your body. Your soul loves the truth. On this journey, you are going to take yourself to the time and place of the root cause of one of your blockages. Continue relaxing, going deeper and deeper into your subconscious mind. You have access to all the information you need in this journey.

Now that you are relaxed, imagine yourself in a beautiful meadow. This meadow is surrounded by trees. There's a gentle breeze rustling the grass blades. You are safe in this meadow. You are at peace. Notice the colors that surround you. Notice the smells of the meadow, the sounds of the meadow. All is well.

In the distance, you notice a gray mist forming. The mist becomes thicker and thicker as it starts rolling towards you. You know this mist is safe. The shimmering, twirling gray mist comes closer and closer to you and finally surrounds you where you cannot see anything - you can only feel that you are safe and secure within the mist.

As the mist is twirling around you, a door appears in front of you. You walk towards the door, opening the door and stepping into a black room. You are inside this room, and you know you are safe. This is the room of transition and transformation. You feel your body transform like you are putting on a costume. You are the same, but your body begins to change inside the room. Your body is changing to the life of the root cause of the blockage that is ready to be healed. The transformation is now complete.

You see the door, you turn the knob and as you open the door, you take a step forward, looking down at your feet. You are now in the time and place that your soul wants you to be in to heal your blockage. What do your feet look like? Do you have shoes on or are you barefoot? What kind of ground are you standing on? Are you male or female? What kind of clothes are you wearing? How old might you be?

Take a look at your surroundings. Are you alone or are there people with you or nearby? Where might you be? Get a sense of who you are in this time and place. Now that you are there, transport yourself to a specific event in this life, the experience that your soul wants you to know, to heal. What is the situation that caused the blockage in this life? Take a moment to observe the event. You are safe and secure as you observe this event. You may be in your body as you experience the event or you may be floating above your body, observing the situation.

Now that you have observed the experience that has caused your blockage, you have a choice. You can choose to change the situation altogether; you can change the meaning of the situation; or can choose something else. What would you like to do? If you want to change the situation, you might go backwards in time a little bit to alter the outcome. If you want to change the situation, go ahead and do so now. If you want to change the meaning of the experience, ask yourself, what is your new understanding of the event that you witnessed or experienced? Do you view it in a new way? How can you change the meaning? Take some time in this life to make any desired changes. You can take yourself backwards and forwards in time as you want and need to view this life and the outcomes. (Pause)

Now that you have had time to explore this life and make any changes you might want to make, fast forward to the end of it. What lessons did you learn that you want to bring back to your current life? How has this life changed for you? Go ahead and leave that body, floating up towards the light. As you're floating, look back down on that body. That is not who you are. It is just a costume you wore, a role you played. Take yourself up to the beautiful white luminescent light. Surround yourself in the white light. You are safe.

Counting backwards from five to one, you will begin to come back to the current time and place. Five, you are bringing back the wisdom of the life you just experienced. Four, you have healed the blockage that revealed itself to you in that life. Three, you are coming back, becoming aware of your consciousness. Two, you are coming back closer and closer, starting to wiggle your fingers and toes. One, you are back to your body. You can slowly open your eyes in your own time. Write down what you experienced in this journey to your past.

Journey to Future Meditation

Get yourself into a comfortable, relaxed position. Close your eyes and take several deep breaths, allowing your mind and body to relax. Melt into the surface below you. Allow yourself to go deeper and deeper into your subconscious mind. You are safe. You are secure. All is well. Become one with your breath. Become one with your surroundings. Imagine a luminous white streaming light above your head. Open up your crown chakra and let the light flow through your body like a waterfall. As the white light flows through every part of your body, it is removing all blocked energy, stuck energy. The white light flows like a river down through your head and out the bottom of your feet, relaxing every part of your body. Your soul loves the truth. On this journey, you are going to take yourself to a future time and place to observe your life situation.

Now that you are relaxed, imagine yourself in a beautiful meadow. This meadow is surrounded by trees. There's a gentle breeze rustling the grass blades. You are safe in this meadow. You are at peace. Notice the colors that surround you. Notice the smells of the meadow, the sounds of the meadow. All is well.

In the distance, you notice a river. As you walk closer to the river, you hear the water moving gently over the rocks. You see a bridge that crosses the river. Walk now to the beginning of the bridge. As you start to cross the bridge, you notice a gray mist start to form over the bridge, getting thicker and thicker. The beautiful shimmering gray mist is welcoming you to step into it. Move towards the mist and let it surround you like a safe, warm blanket. You are safe inside the mist. As you are walking through the mist, over the bridge, time is moving forward. Continue walking, and as you cross to the other side of the riverbank, you are now five years in the future.

What is going on in your life? Where do you live? Who do you live with? Do you have a job, are you retired, or something else? How do you feel? Do you like the life you are living five years in the future? Is there anything that you would like to change? Take some time to explore this future time. (Pause)

Now move yourself to ten years in the future. What is your life like ten years from now? How do you feel? What do you notice? Take some time to explore this future time. (Pause)

Now that you have observed yourself and your life five and ten years in the future, make note of anything specific you want to change in that future. Know that you can change the trajectory of that timeline if you desire by making small shifts in your present life.

When you are ready and in your own time, come back to the here and now and write down what you observed and if there is anything that you want to change.

Ancestral Healing Meditation

Get yourself into a comfortable, relaxed position. Close your eyes and take several deep breaths, allowing your mind and body to relax. Melt into the surface below you. Allow yourself to go deeper and deeper into your subconscious mind. You are safe. You are secure. All is well. Become one with your breath. Become one with your surroundings.

Now that you are relaxed, in your mind's eye, transport yourself to a campfire circle. There is a fire burning in the middle of the circle, a warm, red and orange fire, flickering in the night. Sit down by the fire and get comfortable. You can sit in a chair or on the ground or something else. Stare into the fire, watching the flames dance. Keep your awareness on the flames. You are going to call in your ancestors around the campfire to ask them for guidance and wisdom. They will share with you the root cause of the ancestral issue you want to be healed.

As you are sitting and watching the warm, beautiful fire, think about the blockage or limitation you want to understand, that you want to heal. Know that the ancestors that can help you understand the issues will join you at the campfire.

In the distance, you notice someone coming towards the fire. As they get closer and closer, you begin to make out who they are. Who is this ancestor? What do they look like? What sense do you get from them? Once they are seated at the fire on your left side, go ahead and ask them what they want you to know about the blockage or limitation in the bloodline. What wisdom do they want you to know? (Pause)

You notice another figure in the distance coming toward you, another ancestor that has information to share with you. They come closer and sit by the fire on your right side. Who is this ancestor? What is your observation of them? Ask them what they want to share with you about the blockage or limitation, the wound that resides in the bloodline. (Pause)

Continue looking into the fire, sitting with your ancestors on either side of you. Now another ancestor is joining you at the campfire, sitting on your left side. Who is this person? What do they look like? What do you feel from them? Ask them what they would like to share with you regarding the wound in the bloodline. (Pause)

There is one more ancestor that is waiting to join you and your family at the fire. This ancestor is the original family member that experienced the blockage and kept it held inside of the genetic memory of the bloodline. The ancestor is coming closer and closer, and they are now sitting on your right side. Who is this ancestor, the root of the family issue? What do they look like? Have them tell you or show you what the original experience was that they kept held tight. (Pause)

Now you have four ancestors gathered around the fire, each carrying the wound that has been passed down generation after generation. Imagine each ancestor as a little child. The first ancestor on your right now comes to you and sits on your lap. Put your arms around this little child, infusing them with love. Let them know how special they are, how loved they are. All is well.

Continue having your ancestors, one child at a time, come to receive your love and comfort. Hug them. Let them know how special they are. The experiences they had do not define who they are. It is okay to release the wounds, the blockages and limitations. As they each receive the love from you, the timelines are shifting, changing, healing. The exper-

iences no longer stay trapped in the body, inside the DNA. The emotions are releasing. The bloodline is healed. (Pause)

When you have spent enough time in front of the fire with your ancestors, go ahead and come back to the present time and space, knowing that you have healed the bloodline.

Final thought: Be gentle with yourself as you are healing your past blockages and limitations. Remember that you are human in this incarnation, and you will make mistakes. You can always start again.

"If you aren't good at loving yourself, you will have a difficult time loving anyone, since you'll resent the time and energy you give another person that you aren't even giving to yourself."
– Barbara De Angelis

5

Creating Your Love Environment

"Love yourself for who you are, and trust me, if you are happy from within, you are the most beautiful person, and your smile is your best asset."
—Ileana D'Cruz

At this point in the workbook, you have revealed your blockages and limitations. You are working through the various exercises and methods to heal those wounds. You may think that is all that is needed to stay happy and healthy, but it isn't. Now it is time to create physical, emotional, and spiritual environments that will support and nurture you in your new life, the new you.

Buckminster Fuller once said, "Environment is stronger than willpower." No matter what our intentions, our environments affect us psychologically and physiologically at the subconscious level.

As you are rewiring your brain for the new you, you will want to create environments that naturally support you in this endeavor. I share different methods that will allow you to create supportive physical, emotional and spiritual environments to help you rejuvenate and re-center yourself and to nurture your self-love and happiness.

Physical Environment

Clutter Clearing

Clutter clearing is one of the best things you can do to improve your life. When it comes to creating space for a new relationship, doing the mental work, as you did in the previous exercises, is very important. However, you also need to create physical space for your new love, for example, emptying space in your closets and drawers for them to put their stuff. Once you complete the decluttering process in your bedroom and bathroom, I recommend that you continue the process in other rooms in your home, as well as your garage. This will ensure your entire home environment is supporting you mentally and physically.

Why Clutter Clearing Works

There are numerous scientific studies on how clutter affects us psychologically and physiologically. According to Psychology Today, some of the psychological issues clutter can cause are a decreased sense of wellbeing, unhealthy eating, poorer mental health, less efficient visual processing and less efficient thinking.

The physiological effects of clutter in a space include chaos in the mind, breathing problems, mental confusion and overall discomfort. It also stifles the energy flowing through a room, causing the energy to be stagnant, heavy and oppressive or claustrophobic.

Clutter can drain your energy, both mentally and physically. It causes stress, anxiety and tension. It can make it harder to get a good night's sleep. It can rob you of time because you are unable to find things easily. It can also cause you to spend more money than you would otherwise because you don't know what you have in your home already.

On a visual level, clutter takes away from the beauty of your home. It can detract from an amazing view and distract us from art and décor that might bring us joy and peace.

When a room is clutter free, it feels open and expansive. There is room to move around. It creates possibility and uplifts the spirit. It is calming. You will be more productive in your time. You may shed excess pounds without trying. It will help you to release the past emotionally. It will help you to have more focused mental clarity. It can remove blockages in creativity. It can help with allergies because there are fewer surface areas for dust to collect. It opens you up to opportunity. It can give you more energy and bring happiness to your space.

What is clutter? Clutter can be paperwork/receipts, artwork and photos, accessories and collections, furniture, clothing and shoes, and junk. It can be anything you have too much of.

When you are clearing out your spaces, ask yourself:

- Do I love this?

- Have I used it or worn it in the last two years?

If you answer no to these questions, I strongly encourage you to let the item(s) go. Ask yourself, why am I holding onto this? Out of obligation? Fear? As you release each item, affirm to yourself that you are clearing all that you no longer need from your life.

If your ultimate desire is to find your ideal partner, you will want to spend extra effort in your master bedroom and bathroom.

Step 1 – Clean out your master bedroom closet(s); leave some empty space

Step 2 – Clean out your dresser drawers; leave at least one drawer completely empty

Step 3 – Clean out your personal bathroom; leave some empty space

By creating empty space in your closet, your drawers and in the bathroom cabinet/ closet, you are telling the Universe you have "room" in your life for a partner to come in. You do not have to create the exact space a partner might want or need, but you do want the emptiness to be noticeable to you. Energetically, the Universe will help you to fill in the space. Be patient, though, as this could take some time. Don't fill the empty space back up with your own new items unless you have decided to stay single.

This is one of the strategies I implemented when I was ready for a new partner in my life. It took a little time, but it worked.

Smudging Your Space

What is smudging? It is a process using the smoke from dried herbs that cleanses and clears the air and energy from a space to renew and refresh it. Though some people view this as a "New Age" thing, Native Americans and other indigenous peoples have used smudging as a cleansing and clearing ritual since ancient times. Its benefits are also backed up by modern science (Mohagheghzadeh, Faridi, Shams-Ardakani, Ghasemi, 2006).

There are numerous scientific benefits to smudging your space. It cleanses the air of unwanted bacteria. In fact, scientific studies have found up to 94% of bacteria is killed off for up to twenty-four hours after smudging. It clears the air of dust, pet dander, mold spores, pollen and other allergens. It produces negative ions, which increases overall wellbeing, improves mental focus and memory and increases energy so it can be used as a natural anti-depressant. It also improves sleep patterns by regulating serotonin levels. It calms and relaxes the body, relieving stress and tension.

From a spiritual perspective, smudging can clear negative energy from emotions held in a room, including anger, anxiety, fear, depression and grief. It can cleanse objects that hold negative energy from previous owners. It increases clarity and awareness, heightens wisdom and quickens the senses.

Personally, I have used smudging to clear my home of negative energy after certain people have visited, as well as to rid it of ghosts and spirits experienced by myself and my kids.

Smudging can be done with various herbs including sage, cedar and sweetgrass, depending on your intentions. Sage is used for healing, as well as to bless, cleanse and heal a person, object or house. White sage is for purifying and clearing negative energy. Black sage is for protection. Cedar is used for protection and cleansing. Sweetgrass is used for blessing and reminding us of the feminine essence of the Earth. You may have a local shop that sells smudging herbs, or you can purchase them online.

I recommend you smudge your bedroom and closet once it has been cleared of clutter. It will refresh your space and clear the energy, leaving you with a clean slate.

Beautify Your Bedroom Space

Your bedroom is the main room where romance happens, so you will want to create a bedroom and bathroom space that looks and feels great. In my previous book, *Sacred Soul Spaces: Designing Your Personal Oasis*, I walk you step-by-step through the design process to create a room that nurtures and inspires your dreams, goals and desires. If you want additional information regarding designing a beautiful, intentional space, I suggest you read that as well.

The amount of furniture you have in the space and the placement of the furniture will affect your overall wellbeing, just as the amount of clutter does. You don't want the bedroom to feel too claustrophobic with too much furniture, so make sure it is proportional to the size of the room.

Your bedding is usually the largest accessory item you put in your room, so you want to make sure it is something you love. Make sure your bedding feels good to you, especially if, like me, you're sensitive to the feel of certain fabrics. Consider purchasing new sheets and towels that look and feel good to you as well. This brings fresh energy to your bedroom space and will enhance your happiness in the room. Add in flowers, décor and artwork that inspire you.

Colors for the Bedroom

Different colors affect us psychologically and physiologically on the subconscious level, so it is important to choose carefully while creating your Sacred Soul Bedroom Space. Below, I've grouped colors together based on the overall effect they can have on your environment. Please note that the energy of some colors can be overpowering and will need to be balanced with other colors.

Love, Passion, Romance

Red

If you want to bring passion into the bedroom, red, the color of love, lust and sexuality, will ignite the fire within you. Red stimulates you physiologically, increasing your heart and respiratory rates, enhancing libido, elevating levels of energy and increasing confidence and enthusiasm. Beware of using too much red, however, as it can create hatred and agitation. Because of its high energy, too much may create an environment that is harder to sleep in. A little bit of red in a bedroom can go a long way, so consider using red accessories, pillows, artwork and flowers in the room, rather than painting your walls that color. Green is a great color to use to counteract the effects of too much red in a room.

Pink

Pink is a color of unconditional love and understanding. It is feminine and romantic, thoughtful and caring. It has a gentle, loving energy. It helps put people in touch with their nurturing side, whether giving or receiving. When used too much, pink can be seen as immature and girlish, so if you are wanting to attract a partner into your life, you may want to limit how much pink is in your room, unless it is a darker pink, like magenta. Deeper pinks exhibit more passion and energy. Pink is a good color for bedrooms when you want to create love and comfort.

Magenta

Magenta uplifts the spirits and promotes compassion and kindness. It represents universal love. It creates happiness, contentment, cheerfulness and appreciation for what you have. It increases dream activity and helps to turn those dreams into reality. It is innovative and imaginative. Too much magenta can trigger depression and despair in some people and may not be good for introverts and those with chronic depression. Green is a good balance color to tone down magenta energy.

Purple

Purple inspires unconditional and selfless love. It also encourages sensitivity and compassion, though that makes it vulnerable to illness. It is feminine and romantic. It is known for stimulating creativity and originality in artists and dreamers. That said, large amounts of purple can trigger depression and moodiness, particularly in those that are susceptible to depressed states. Adding in small bursts of purple into your home décor can be a way to bring the color in without overdoing it.

Teal

Teal helps to build self-esteem and self-love. It enhances empathy and caring. It's a friendly, happy color that opens communication between the heart and spoken word. It can alleviate feelings of loneliness. Too much teal may lead to an overactive mind and create emotional imbalance. Too little may cause a withholding of emotions.

Rest, Relaxation, Health

Green

Green is the color of balance, harmony and growth. It is an emotionally positive color, which gives us the ability to love and nurture others and ourselves unconditionally. It is the color of health and balances the heart and the emotions. It restores depleted energy and restores a sense of wellbeing. It pairs well with most, if not all other colors.

Teal

Teal has the calm tranquility of blue, the growth and balance of green, and the uplifting energy of yellow. It controls and heals the emotions by creating emotional balance and stability. It calms the nervous system and helps in decision-making, including in emergency situations. It gives control over self-expression and builds confidence. It encourages inner healing, recharges the spirit in times of mental stress, and can alleviate feelings of loneliness.

Blue

Blue promotes both physical and mental relaxation, can reduce stress and creates a sense of calmness, relaxation and order. It slows down the metabolism. This color is great for bedrooms where people want ease and peace. For a calm, relaxing feeling in the bedroom, you might try a softer blue with or without a hint of green in it. The paler the blue, the more freedom we feel.

Purple

Purple represents the imagination, dreams and the future. It promotes harmony of mind and emotions and supports the practice of meditation. Soft purple tones are great in rooms for relaxation.

Joy, Cheer, Optimism

Orange

Orange creates happiness and optimism. It uplifts us in a way other colors do not. It gives us the freedom to be ourselves. It helps us overcome grief and bounce back from disappointments. It also keeps us motivated and inspires a positive outlook on life.

Yellow

Yellow can be uplifting, offering hope, fun and cheerfulness. It creates enthusiasm for life and can generate optimism and confidence. It also helps to inspire new ideas and new ways of doing things from the practical side of the brain. On the downside, yellow can create anxiety and agitation because it is a fast-moving color. It is the most difficult color for the eye to take in and can be overpowering if overused. Adding yellow accents to a room is easier than picking the perfect yellow paint.

Greenery for the Bedroom

One way to make your Sacred Soul Bedroom look and feel amazing is to bring the outside in. Real plants and flowers bring energy into a room, improving air quality and the overall feng shui. Note that some plants are known for special properties. Those listed below have multiple properties, so I am classifying them based on their most important quality for the bedroom.

Plants for Love

- **Jasmine** – attracts positive energy; strengthens relationships and builds romance; and attracts love and money. Jasmine is an aphrodisiac; encourages prophetic dreams; soothes stress and provides energy. Place in a south-facing window.

🌱 **Orchid** – attracts positive energy and improves the energy of a home and the lives of its inhabitants; attracts love; soothes the soul; and deepens friendships. Orchids are associated with fertility and virility. They are good in a bedroom as they release oxygen at night.

🌱 **Basil** – clears air of negative energy and attracts positive energy to the home. It is also an antioxidant with antibacterial, anti-fungal and anti-in-flammatory properties. Basil brings love, passion, wealth and luck. Place in full sun in north, east or northeastern area of home.

🌱 **Miniature Roses** - Each rose color has its own meaning:
- White with red details – passion and devotion
- Pink – romantic love, sweetness, fun, play
- Fuchsia – lust for life, self-love, deep love and acceptance of the physical body
- Red – passionate, deep, true love

Plants for Restful Sleep and Healing

🌱 **Peace Lily** – has spiritual, mental and physical benefits; improves flow of energy in the home; purifies air and neutralizes harmful indoor gases. Good in bedrooms for tranquility and restful sleep; grows well in shaded or dark environments.

🌱 **Rosemary** – promotes mental and physical wellbeing; purifies air to keep free of toxins; uplifts mood; reduces fatigue and anxiety; improves memory; brings inner peace; helps with sleep; attracts love and encourages lust. Prefers a sunny window.

🌱 **Lavender** – elevates mood; calms and relaxes; helps with sleep; helps alleviate headaches.

🌱 **Miniature Roses** – Each rose color has its own meaning:
- White – purifying and healing, positive energy
- Peach – peace, spirituality and friendship
- Lavender – spirituality

Once you have cleared your clutter, created empty space in your closet and drawers and designed a bedroom that supports your dreams and desires, make a conscious effort to upkeep the space. Don't allow your bedroom sanctuary to become overwhelmed with clutter and messiness. Make your bed daily. Hang up your towels neatly after using them, rather than tossing them on the floor. Treat your bedroom with the same respect you treat yourself.

Emotional Environment

There are numerous methods you can use to create and upkeep your emotional environment to its optimal status. In this section, I share with you the exercises and methods I use. Feel free to use any or all of these that resonate with you. If you have other activities you like, you can incorporate those into your routine as well.

Daily gratitude list

Writing out a daily gratitude list is a transformational exercise. It helps to keep you focused on what you are grateful for in your life rather than being bogged down by the negative things that pop up for you. You can do this any time of the day or night. You may have a particular time you can commit to, which is the most important thing. The key to the success is to do it daily, or as often as you can. When your mind focuses on positive things, you are resonating at a higher frequency, which helps to create more positive things in your life.

Below I share two ways to do this, but there are many others. Do what works for you.

Method 1: Each night before bed, write down at least five things you are grateful for that happened that particular day. There may be some days where you have a long list and other days where you struggle to come up with even one thing. Commit to five grateful things, no matter how small they are. For example, if all you did was get out of bed that day, it is a win and something to be grateful for.

Method 2: At some point in the day, write out a pre-emptive gratitude list. These are the things you want to create in your life. Write them as if they have already happened and you are thankful for them. For instance, if I wanted to create attracting my ideal partner, I might write out: I am grateful for attracting the love of my life who supports and nurtures me.

Exercise Routine

I strongly recommend that you create an exercise routine that works for you and your schedule. Exercising is not only good for keeping in good physical condition, it also moves energy and releases endorphins to increase your sense of well-being. Working out also clears the mind and works wonders for your emotional body. Your regimen could be as simple as walking three to five times a week, or it could be more extensive, such as attending classes, hiring a personal trainer, or any other physical activity you enjoy. Regular exercise will help keep you healthy and help you to feel better about yourself and how your body looks and acts.

Self-care

We live in a fast-paced world that encourages us to be busy around the clock, and it's easy to feel bogged down by responsibilities. It does not have to be this way, so long as we make time to fulfill our responsibility to ourselves. Take me, for example. I'm a mother of two younger children. I run two businesses. I have a husband. I have close friends and other people I interact with on a regular basis. Having a regular self-care practice keeps me sane. It took me many years to figure out I could not take care of others if I was not taking care of myself.

Create a self-care routine you love and are excited about. It might be getting regular massages. It could be getting manicures and pedicures. Maybe you like yoga. There might be a local meditation group you join. Whatever it is, start a routine and make it a priority in your schedule. When you take care of yourself you will feel better emotionally; you will also be in a better place when meeting new people.

Hang out with Friends

Whether you have one or two close friends or a larger social circle, make time to spend quality time with them. It could be hosting dinner parties, going out to dinner, or participating in other group activities. Whatever it is, carve out time in your schedule to interact with your friends. Make sure these people uplift you. You don't want to be in an environment with those who are negative and suck you into their drama-filled worlds.

Tapping and Clearing

When you find yourself getting caught up in an emotional wave, there are various ways to help you release those emotions. One modality that has become more well-known in recent years is the Emotional Freedom Technique (EFT), or tapping. There are books that can teach you how to tap, such as Nick Ortner's, *The Tapping Solution*. There are also practitioners who can work with you to clear out your emotions using this method.

Treat Yourself as You Want to be Treated

One thing I want you to do no matter what else you do for yourself emotionally is to treat yourself the way you want others to treat you. If you are constantly putting yourself down, mentally or physically, you are creating an environment that invites others to do the same to you. If you treat yourself well with healthy mind and body talk, you will be able to see and hear when others are not treating you well, and you can get away from them. This is all about having strong boundaries and keeping them. Don't let others cross your boundaries and get away with it.

What Other People Think of Me is None of My Business

One of the most profound lessons I learned in my Al-Anon meetings is what other people think of me is none of my business; it was also one of the most challenging. I had been a people-pleaser my entire life, wanting everyone to think I was worthy and loveable. What

I had to learn is the love and worthiness had to come from within me; only then would I be able to know and fully feel the love of others. I had to come to terms with the fact not everyone was going to like me, and that was okay. My job was to be authentic with myself and others. If I was truthful and authentic in my words and actions, then I could have peace of mind that what others think didn't matter. If I was doing or saying something that wasn't truly me, then I had to examine it and change it for myself, not because others wanted me to.

It took years to come to terms with this with my second ex-husband. He had never liked my spiritual side and thought, given my science background, that I should be more logical and skeptical. During the majority of our relationship, I largely suppressed my spirituality. He was so fearful of such ideas, he tried to control what I said to the kids about them. Now that we are divorced, he doesn't have the control. He still judges me for what I talk about with the kids, but his opinion of me and my woo-woo ideology is irrelevant to me. It is none of my business.

Think about people who may judge you or have opinions of you that you don't like very much. Now tell yourself that what they think of you is none of your business. Keep practicing this until it becomes natural.

Empath "Protection" – Blue Light/Archangel Michael

As empaths, we feel what others feel. Oftentimes we are not aware that the emotions we are experiencing are not actually our own feelings, so we internalize them and make them our own. If you notice yourself getting caught up in an emotional wave that is not yours, think about yourself as a willow tree. The emotions are like the breeze blowing through your branches. The leaves dance in the wind, but the breeze passes. The emotions come into your body and pass through like the breeze. Don't mistake the emotions for the leaves; rather, they are simply rustling the leaves.

My mentor and coach, Sunny Dawn Johnston, taught me an easy-to-do practice that has helped me protect my energy field *before* I come into contact with other people. If you are an empath like I am, this one technique, practiced daily, will dramatically impact your emotional world in a good way. I call on Archangel Michael and his blue shield of light to surround my body to maintain my energy and keep out others' energy, both seen and unseen. I then imagine a blue sphere of light around my body. This is not a protection invocation, per se, but a way to summon and strengthen my own energy.

Do this invocation when you first wake up. This way it becomes a daily practice and you will be ready to interact with people, including those in your home, without taking on their emotions.

Coaching

I have had numerous life and business coaches over the years, and it is one of the best things I have done for myself, with lasting effects. I continue to hire coaches to this day because it helps keep me in check with what I am doing and how I am interacting in the world.

If you decide to work with a coach, my recommendation is that you choose someone who has done what you want to accomplish or has the tools to help you accomplish your dreams and goals. For business, I hire those who have been more successful than me. For life, I hire those who live a life I admire and want to emulate. Not all coaches are created equal.

Continue Going Deeper and Deeper

Even when you think you are healthy and maintaining your emotional body, new experiences and situations will come up that need to be assessed and moved through. You are like an onion with many layers, so as you work through something, it may come up again at a different time with a deeper element to it, like a spiral. Keep going deeper and deeper into yourself to heal those parts of you that are injured.

Spiritual Environment

Spirituality and its practices are not "one size fits all," but a personal experience unique to each individual. In this section, I share what has worked for me. You may have other ways you maintain your spiritual environment. There is no right or wrong here. Just do it.

Sacred Soul Love Vision Board

Vision boards are a powerful manifesting tool that help you visualize your goals and dreams on a daily basis. Creating a vision board amplifies your intentions and energizes the space in which you place it. When you are in this space and looking at your board, you are able to generate more energy toward your dreams, thus bringing them into reality.

Boards can be made for your overall intention for your life, as well as for specific areas, such as health/wellness, career/money or love/relationships. My recommendation is to have one dedicated to love.

For those who have never made a vision board before, it is actually quite simple. You will need a few materials, including a thick poster board to be used as the base. You can determine if a small or large board will work best for your dreams. I personally like the large ones, so I can fit more images onto the space. You will also need some adhesive. I found that glue sticks work really well for affixing the images onto the board.

Using magazines, pictures and other paper-based materials, cut or tear out words and images that symbolize your dreams, what you want to manifest and how you want to feel. If you don't have a pile of magazines at your disposal, you can ask to borrow from friends and relatives if they have desired titles and are okay with you tearing them up. You might need to purchase some magazines that have the types of words and images that speak to you. You can also print out images from the Internet.

Once you have your images and words ready, it is time to place them on the board. Some people like to pre-place everything before they start gluing. Other people glue as they go. There is no right or wrong way to do this. You want to be able to see all of your intentions, so make sure you don't cover up words with larger images. You can layer the words onto the images. Having some empty space is okay. I like using a poster board with some color in the background, so if I do end up with a bit of empty space, the background color fills it.

If you are creating a vision board with multiple intentions, consider segmenting certain areas of the board for particular areas of your life. You can be as organized as you like or as abstract and random as you like. Again, there is no wrong way to do this. Trust your intuition on how to create your board for your ultimate outcome.

Creating a vision board can be done once a year or several times a year. Do what calls to you. The time and focus that goes into creating your board helps you to hold your intention in your mind's eye during the process.

Once you have completed your board, hang it in a prominent place where you will see it each day. The more time your mind spends taking in the images on the board, the more likely your subconscious mind is to call your desires into being.

Create a Love Altar

Altars have traditionally been found in Eastern cultures as well as in some Christian sects. With yoga and meditation practices on the rise in Western society, altars are growing more popular. The purpose of creating an altar is to reinforce the intentions of your Sacred Soul Love by calling in spiritual energies. I recommend using objects representing love.

To create an altar, the first step is to find a location in your home where it will be visible to you. It could be in a corner of a room, on top of a table or dresser, or even on a bookshelf. Use your intuition to figure out where you want the altar to be located.

Once you have decided on the location, select objects representing love for the altar. Examples of things to include would be a light source, such as a candle or a salt lamp; fresh flowers or herbs; inspirational books; crystals/stones; photos of loved ones or spiritual figures; elements from nature (shells, rocks, feathers, coral, sticks, etc.) and bells or chimes. Hold the object in your hand to see if it speaks to you about belonging on the altar. Only use items that resonate with the energy you want to create.

Now that you have chosen your objects, it is time to arrange them in the altar space. If using a flat surface, such as a table, place the taller items in the back with shorter objects in the front. Rearrange until you are happy with the positioning of the objects.

The final step is to bless the altar by saying words of gratitude or a prayer. It does not have to be long. The most important thing is the intention you are infusing into your altar with your thoughts.

Once you have the altar set up and blessed, use it in a daily ritual to enhance its energy. Over time, you will be compelled to shift items around on your altar and even change what objects you have on it. Trust your intuition. You will know when it is time for modification.

Mantras & Affirmations

An effective practice that can help you connect to your spiritual self and rewire your brain is saying mantras or affirmations. A mantra can be a single word or sound repeated over and over to aid in concentration for meditation, such as in the Hindu and Buddhist traditions. They are sacred and practiced in a devotional, spiritual way. Affirmations are statements or slogans repeated frequently. They are motivational, helping you to overcome the negative thoughts that are currently limiting you. Some people use the terms *mantra* and *affirmation* interchangeably.

When you are creating your own affirmation or manta, there are some important elements you will want to include for them to be effective. Your affirmation must be in the present tense, such as "I am . . ."; "I have . . ."; "I trust . . ." and so on. By writing or saying the affirmation in the present tense, you are creating the energy of those words for you now. The brain responds to present tense statements. Your affirmation must only include positive words to work effectively. You do not want to use words like "don't" and "can't" because in doing so you may actually create more of what you don't want. Your affirmation needs to be written or spoken as the truth of the situation, rather than using wishy-washy words like "might" and "could."

Once you have one or more affirmations, it is imperative that you repeat it/them to yourself each day, throughout the day. You might want to write your affirmation on a piece of paper and put in a place you see frequently such as in your car, on your bathroom mirror or at your office. To strengthen the affirmation, you can put a physical touch with it, such as done in the EFT tapping technique. This creates muscle memory with the affirmation, so it is fully incorporated into your body and mind. Say it out loud with energy and intention multiple times a day. Meditate on it with or without a mala. You can also write it out multiple times in a row, sort of like writing lines on a chalkboard in school.

Powerful Affirmations:

I am a light to the world

I remember who I am

I am a divine being

Love is all there is

I share my gifts with the world

I manifest my desires effortlessly

I am filled with love and joy

I am in the flow with the Universe

My soul loves the truth

I live a passion-filled life

I am neutral in my emotions and let go of the outcome

I am abundant and prosperous in all areas of my life

I am a whole and healthy person

I consciously create my reality

I continue to learn and grow in self-awareness

I am honest and authentic in all of my interactions with myself and others

I am the source of my happiness, love, approval and safety

I am an excellent giver and receiver

I am patient and gentle with myself

I live in gratitude

What other people think of me is none of my business

I am open and expansive

Self-love is true love

I have perfect health in mind, body and spirit

I am an inspiration to myself and others

I stand in my full power

I am enough for myself

I am beautiful at any age, size or shape

I am love

I create strong boundaries and keep them

I am worthy

I am free to be my authentic self

I am comfortable in my own skin

I treat myself as I want others to treat me

I honor and cherish myself

I take full responsibility for the circumstances of my life

I surround myself with a supportive environment

I am a phoenix rising from the ashes

I value and respect myself

I forgive myself and others for experiences of the past, present and future

I learn the lessons and gain the wisdom

I continue to peel back the layers to reveal the essence of who I truly am

I release my blocks and limitations

I heal my ancestral bloodline

I hear and trust my inner wisdom

Malas with Mantras

I recommend using a mala in your meditation with your mantra or affirmation, so long as it resonates with you. Malas help focus the mind when you are reciting the words. Traditional malas are necklace-like strands of beads that have 108 smaller beads plus one additional larger "guru" bead. Shorter malas have either 54 beads or 27 beads, plus the guru bead.

When you are working with your mala, use only one mantra or affirmation for each session. Sit comfortably with your eyes closed and get yourself aligned with your intention. Hold the mala in your right hand with the beads in between your index and middle fingers. Starting at the guru bead, you use your thumb to pull each bead toward you as you recite the mantra/affirmation, for a total of 108 (54 or 27) times, until you reach the guru bead again.

Malas can be made out of a variety of different types of beads. I personally love my malas to be made from natural crystals and stones, so I also get the benefits of those stones. They can help to amplify your intentions when reciting your affirmations and mantras. Every stone has different energy and meaning, so you can combine stones to incorporate a few meanings into the mala, or you may want to keep it simpler with one stone type.

Love Stones and Crystals

Here are just some of the stones that carry the energy of love and healing in them.

Amazonite – connects us to our inner power, intuitive wisdom, and universal love. It also boosts self-love, boosts metabolism, restores one's faith in life, and encourages one to spread their wings and fly.

Color: pale blue-green

Carnelian – grounds, balances, and heals relationships; manifests thoughts into the physical; offers protection

Color: deep orange

Celestine – brings calmness and harmony; transmutes pain into love and light; and assists with achieving a higher level of consciousness and personal truth

Color: light blue

Chrysocolla – promotes healing of the heart and emotions; gives you great inner strength in hard times

Color: light blue to blue green

Cobalto Calcite – heals emotions and fosters unconditional love, compassion and forgiveness. Cobalto Calcite also cultivates self-love, mends broken hearts, heals grief, speeds the healing process, manifests abundance, and reduces stress.

Color: pink to crimson

Desert Rose – enhances feelings of wellbeing and understanding your own personal value in the Universe

Color: brown, tan, white and soft yellow

Diamond – a stone of clarity, communication and commitment. Diamond enhances prosperity, spirituality and love.

Color: clear, blue, pink and yellow

Emerald – a stone of successful love, loyalty and bliss. Emerald strengthens memory and focus, and increases inner knowing, truth and discernment. It also deepens spirituality and consciousness.

Color: green

Kunzite – connects us to the infinite source of love and facilitates purification on all levels. Kunzite enhances the expression of self-love, unconditional love and romantic love; it also removes obstacles from one's path, dissolves negativity, clears and protects the auric field, and inspires openness.

Color: pale pink, lavender, clear, yellow, and green

Lemurian Quartz – excellent for dream work and deep heart connections. Lemurian Quartz inspires unconditional love for the Divine and each other; it also deepens the connection to all humanity and offers a circle of light protection, connects you to ancient information from past civilizations, aids in telepathy, and promotes self-confidence.

Color: clear with light-encoded horizontal lines

Lepidolite – great for stress reduction. Lepidolite allows one to transition out of difficult challenges in life, inspires childlike love and acceptance, and strengthens the discovery of Higher Self.

Color: lavender to violet purple with sparkling specks

Pink Tourmaline – inspires unconditional love and forgiveness of self and others, as well as grace, gentleness, compassion and kindness

Color: pale pink

Rhodochrosite – helps create a balanced, loving approach to life and eases moments of change

Color: creamy pink and white

Rhodonite – expands the heart chakra, opens one to unconditional love and increases service to mankind. Rhodonite also inspires generosity of spirit and self-love. It calms, eases anger, and brings emotional balance and confidence; it also enhances passionate love; mends a broken heart; and heals trauma and abuse.

Color: pale pink with some black striations

Rose Quartz – a healing crystal that enhances self-love, beloved purity of self and others, and unconditional love. It nurtures.

Color: pink

Ruby – strengthens leadership, power, protection and detoxification. It also strengthens love.

Color: deep red, pink, magenta

Sodalite – manifests your ability to find your soulmate. It fosters companionship, opens heart to the impossible, and enhances self-esteem and trust in others.

Color: deep blue with white veins

Meditation and Visualization

There are many different ways to meditate. You can quiet your mind. You can be led on a meditative journey. You can focus on specific dreams and goals. You can say mantras or affirmations while meditating.

I personally use different meditation techniques for specific intentions. When I am stressed or anxious, I like to put on meditative music and quiet my mind. When I want to manifest something specific, I use visualization in my meditation. When I want to get an answer about a specific question, I like doing guided meditative journeys.

One technique I learned many years ago at the spiritual school I was attending is how to create your day. It was later explained by Dr. Joe Dispenza in the 2004 movie, *What the Bleep Do We Know!?* and has gained in popularity ever since. To briefly summarize the method, while in a meditative state, you consciously focus on what you want to create for that specific day. You can visualize and say affirmations in your mind. Say each affirmation slowly and consciously three times. You can also create images in your mind representing what you want to create. Hold the image in your mind's eye for as long as you can. Feel the emotion of what it would be like to have already manifested your desire. You can have several things you want to create for your day. Be fully present with each one. Your mind doesn't know the difference between experiences you have with your eyes open and those you have with them shut, so the more real you can make the visualizations in your mind, the more likely your brain will wire to the new pattern and create the reality.

With meditation, the more you do it, the easier it gets. It helps calm and clear the mind to keep you in a healthy spiritual environment.

Final thought: Environment is stronger than willpower. What ways will you commit to supporting your physical, emotional and spiritual environments? Journal in this space below or on a separate sheet of paper or journal.

"You yourself, as much as anybody in the entire universe, deserves your love and affection."
— Buddha

6

Learning to Hear and Trust Your Inner Wisdom

"When you adopt the viewpoint that there is nothing that exists that is not part of you, that there is no one who exists who is not part of you, that any judgment you make is self-judgment, that any criticism you level is self-criticism, you will wisely extend to yourself an unconditional love that will be the light of the world."
– Harry Palmer

Learning to hear and trust your inner wisdom is paramount to your overall happiness in life. When you listen to your own knowingness, you will be able to determine what people and situations are right for you, and those that are not. You will make empowering decisions. You will be in control of your life. You will know what the right answer is for you and your situation despite what others may tell you or claim to know. Ultimately, you will gain self-power. The more you know and understand yourself, the more confident you will be in all areas of your life.

As with all things, there is more than one way to discover the answers from within. I am going to cover the techniques and modalities I have personally used. You may or may not be familiar with some of these. Use the method or methods that work best for you.

In addition to our own wisdom, we have the ability to work with other dimensional beings who are there to guide and support us. These include spirit guides, angels, animals, galactic entities and other messengers. In this chapter, I share ways to connect with these other dimensional beings. I also focus on modalities that will help you get answers from external sources that are true to you. It's all about knowing yourself and how you operate.

Self-Knowing Answers

Oftentimes, society and conditioning make us think we have to behave and perform in a certain way. However, if we are true to ourselves and our inner knowingness, we can live a much easier life in the flow of the Universe. Here are some ways you can get to the root of your inner wisdom so you can decide whether or not something is right for you.

Human Design

Human Design, a modality founded by Ra Uru Hu, combines the ideologies of Western Astrology, the Hindu Chakra system, the Kabbalah Tree of Life, the I Ching, Genetics and Quantum Mechanics. I love this method so much I decided to train in it to help myself and my clients understand the natural design we all have and how to work with it in our lives for ease and flow.

In Human Design, each person has a specific blueprint for this particular life. This includes the way each of us naturally gets an answer to a question so it is the correct answer for us. We are taught to use the mind and logic to make our decisions, but when we override our natural response system to listen to the mind, we often make decisions that turn out to be "wrong" for us. I use the word "wrong" to reflect that we make decisions that go against our greatest good. In reality, there really is no right or wrong. Some decisions take us down a path that may take longer to learn the lessons, and hopefully we will gain the wisdom from those tough decisions.

Think about a time when you instinctively knew something was not right, then let your mind convince you otherwise. You used contrary evidence to continue down the path and it ended up poorly.

An example from my life was when I decided to marry my first husband. Even though my inner knowingness told me it would not last and that I needed to run the other way, my mind, fear and codependency convinced me to move forward. I went ahead with the wedding, only to end the marriage when my daughter was seven months old.

When a Human Design chart is created, one of the crucial aspects is how each person gets to their Yes, No or Not Now; this is termed "Inner Authority." I summarize the different Inner Authorities below. To determine what your specific Inner Authority is, you can run a chart for free on either of the following websites. All you need is your birth date, birth time and location of birth to create an accurate Human Design chart.

https://www.humandesignamerica.com/chart

https://www.jovianarchive.com/Get_Your_Chart

Splenic Authority – "Instant Decisions" - When you have Splenic Authority, your decisions are made as a very quiet spark of knowing through your intuition. You may not know why that is your answer in that particular moment, but you must learn to listen for it and trust it. It will not steer you wrong. You have the ability to make instantaneous or "snap" decisions.

Sacral Authority – "Follow Your Gut" - When you have Sacral Authority, your decisions are made in the gut with a verbal *uh-huh* for yes or *uh-uh* for no or not now. To get the answer, it has to come in the form of a question from an outside source. A good strategy to use for big questions is to have a trusted friend ask you questions about the situation, so you can listen for your answer in your gut. Yes/no questions are best for this authority type.

Emotional Authority – "Be Emotionally Clear" - When you have Emotional Authority, your decisions are made after you go through a roller coaster ride of emotions about the situation. This could take a few minutes, hours, days or even a month to process the emotions. Your answer comes in the stillness at the end of the emotional highs and lows. If you make a decision before your emotional processing is complete, you are likely to make a decision that is more challenging for you.

Heart Authority – "Do What You Want" - If your heart wants it, it is your job to make it happen. It is straightforward and direct. What is your heart's desire? If your heart is not in it, the answer is NO. Think about what is in it for you.

Self-Authority – "Be True to Yourself" - Decisions are made by "knowing," which can be quite subtle sometimes. Your answer will be an innate knowing you can't explain. Listen to what you say, as there is truth in the words you speak.

Outer Authority – "Accessing Intelligence" - Your decisions are made through an external process. Ideas must be researched and fully thought through over a period of time. Usually a lunar cycle of twenty-nine days is the recommended amount of time to process the information for you to make an informed decision.

For more information on Inner Authority as it relates to Human Design, I recommend reading *Human Design: Discover the Person You Were Born to Be* by Chetan Parkyn and *The Definitive Book of Human Design: The Science of Differentiation* by Lynda Bunnell and Ra Uru Hu. Trusting your personal authority and being guided by it is important for major decisions in your life.

Pendulum Work

Pendulums work under the assumption that we can access answers from our own inner wisdom and the Universe. They indicate answers by moving backwards and forwards, side to side or in a circular motion. There are two ways I personally use the pendulum method to get an answer to a question: external pendulum and human pendulum. If you have not done pendulum work, it may take time for you to be able to relax your mind enough for it to work. Don't give up if you don't get an answer the first time. Keep practicing. Over time, it will become more natural to you.

External pendulum

An external pendulum is a weighted object, usually on a string or chain of some sort. My method of using the external pendulum is to hold the chain of the pendulum in one hand, keeping it completely still. I hold my other hand a few inches below the free hanging, weighted part of the pendulum. To have a baseline, with my mind clear and relaxed, I ask the pendulum to show me what a yes looks like. It will begin to move in a certain direction back and forth. I stop it to get it back to neutral. I then ask it to show me what a no looks like. It will move in a different direction from the yes. I again neutralize it and ask to show me what a maybe looks like. It moves in a different direction from the yes and the no. Once the baseline is established, I ask it only yes and no questions. I make sure I don't put any energy into the outcome of the answer. I stay neutral and clear so I can get the accurate answer for myself.

Human pendulum

The human pendulum method is based on the same principle as the external pendulum, but instead of using an external object, I use my body as the pendulum. For this technique, I stand with my feet roughly shoulder width apart with my knees relaxed. I let my arms hang loosely at my sides and gently tilt my head forward to relax my neck. I close my eyes and clear my mind. I establish my baseline of yes, no and maybe. I first ask to show me a yes. My body will sway or move in a specific direction. I neutralize my body, re-center and ask to show me a no. My body sways or moves in a different direction it did for the yes. I repeat the process to determine what a maybe feels like. Once I know the baseline, I can ask myself yes and no questions. I have to be completely neutral about the answer for it to work properly.

Muscle Testing

Muscle testing, scientifically known as applied kinesiology, is another method used to answer yes/no questions. It is based on the premise that the body is a computer and will give you information you need by asking specific questions. There are numerous ways to do muscle testing, so choose one that works best for you. You can learn how to test yourself, or you may have another person test you for the answers.

One way to have a person test for you is by using your arm. Hold your arm out to your side at shoulder level and hold strong. The other person will put one hand on your opposite shoulder for balance and the other hand gently resting on your outstretched forearm. They will ask you a question, either out loud or in their head and then push down on your outstretched arm, while you resist them by trying to keep it at shoulder height. With a yes answer, you will be able to hold your arm strong against their pressing down. With a no answer, your arm will go weak and they will be able to press your arm downward without difficulty.

To test yourself using this method, you can use your hands. To do this, with your less dominant hand, press together your thumb and ring finger, making a circle. With the pointer finger on your other hand inside the circle of your fingers, you can ask yes and no questions, one at a time. With the pointer finger, you want to make a swift strong movement to try to break through the circle of your other fingers. If your fingers stay strong and don't break apart, that is the yes. If your fingers break apart, that is the no. This is a discrete way to test when you want to get to an answer without people noticing.

Oracle Cards

Oracle cards, including tarot cards, can be used to ask questions for guidance on specific issues. One thing to note about card readings is the answers given are not set in stone. They are a reflection of what the likely path will lead to, based on where you are in your life at a particular moment in time. You have free will to change your direction if you don't like the answers you get.

There are so many different oracle card decks, it can be overwhelming to a novice. My recommendation is to pick a deck you are innately drawn to. Start with one deck. You can always add on additional decks as you feel the call to do so. Each oracle card deck will likely have a booklet that comes with it to explain how those particular cards work and how to ask questions. They will give a brief synopsis on what each card represents. It is up to you how you interpret the card or cards for yourself and your situation. One thing I have learned over time in working with different card decks is that the cards never lie. There is always a reason why you pick a particular card. Even if you don't understand the meaning in the moment, if you contemplate or meditate on it, the information will become clearer to you.

For my particular oracle card practice, I choose a deck I am drawn to from my collection for that specific day. I shuffle the cards, asking for what I need to know for my highest good. Once I have cut the deck and spread them out, I choose the card I am drawn to, knowing and trusting it will tell me what I need to be aware of or know for that day. I also use the cards when I have specific questions I want to ask. Just like with the other techniques I have shared so far, the important thing is for me to be neutral to the answer I receive.

Meditation and Dreaming

If we have questions we want answered, we can get answers during our meditations and through our dreams if we allow our mind to relax and get our ego self out of the way. It may take practice to learn to hear or see the answers that come to you. The answer may be loud and clear, or it may flutter into your mind and pass quickly. Trust your knowingness.

In your dreams, you may receive symbols that you will want to decipher when you wake up. You will forget the details of the dream within ten minutes of waking, so I recommend keeping a journal next to your bed so you can write it down immediately. To activate your dreams, make an intention before you go to sleep that your dreams will provide answers and you will remember them upon waking.

External Answers

Psychics

If you do not trust the answers you are getting with the self-testing methods I have described, you may choose to get answers from those with developed psychic ability. Everyone has innate psychic ability, but some people have developed their skill and are more open than others.

When you are choosing a psychic you want to make sure you get a good feeling about them. If you don't know any psychics, you can always ask friends and family for referrals to people they trust.

A good psychic will be able to give you answers. Similar to the oracle cards, the information coming to them is based on the current path you are on in your life. You can make shifts in the trajectory of some predictions if you don't like the answer. That said, some answers you don't like can actually turn out to be for your greatest good. You may really want to hear a yes about a particular situation. If you get a no, trust that something better is headed your way.

Numerology and Astrology

Numerology and Astrology are two other modalities that can help answer questions about your life. Unless you are well-trained in these methods, it is best to seek help from professionals. At a basic level, they can be used to understand the underlying nature of who you are in this particular life and what themes you are here to learn, similar to Human Design. When you go deeper, they can provide information about what is going on in your life in the present time and what might be likely to happen in the upcoming days, months and years, based on your chart. They both use your specific birthdate (and time and place for Astrology) to generate your individual chart.

While Numerology and Astrology provide information about the influences present in your life at certain times, they don't have the ability to answer all of the questions you may have. If you choose to use these methods, I recommend using them in conjunction with other decision-making techniques.

Scientific Hand Analysis

Scientific Hand Analysis is a modality that examines the lines in the hands as well as the fingerprints. It is another diagnostic tool about who you were born to be, similar to Human Design, Numerology and Astrology. While it may not be able to answer specific, real-time questions, it can answer your broader questions about life. Your fingerprints never change, so they represent the soul and what it came to learn. The lines in the hand can and do change throughout your life, so they represent what is going on in the moment.

I had a professional hand analysis done several years ago, and the information I learned about myself completely altered my trajectory at the time. It was the spark I needed to get back to my spiritual roots and start a new path in spiritual coaching.

Messages and Support from other Entities and Dimensions

When you feel like you want and need extra support in your life, you can reach out to your support team from beyond. You can get guidance and messages pertinent to your life.

Spirit guides and messengers are constantly surrounding you and available for you to access their wisdom and knowledge. If you haven't connected with your guides and messengers, guided journeys are a great way to tap into their energy and information. We all have multiple guides and messengers specifically assigned to us. Some are there for a one-time event or for a short time. Others are there throughout your life. They can be loved ones who have passed on, living relatives or friends, past life entities, interdimensional beings, spirit animals, angels and so on.

Every time I have done a meditative journey, I have a new guide there to share wisdom and support me through the experience. Each has a message I need to hear, a gift to remind me of the journey and my interaction with them or something else extraordinary that adds to my overall wellbeing in this life. It connects me to the greater consciousness of existence beyond this human experience.

Spirit Animal Guides and Messengers

I have had a strong connection with animals since I was a child. It took many years before I understood what spirit animals were and was guided to discover my spirit animal. Since then, I have come to understand my connection to several animals and their meaning and inspiration in my life.

In the last several years, I have been attuned to animal messengers coming across my path. Sometimes they come once, and I get the message. Other times they have to show up several days in a row for me to notice.

To give you an example, I started noticing signs – in this case, spiders - the week before I went to California to complete my Past Life Regression training with Denise Linn. Three days in a row there were spiders in different areas of my home. This was highly unusual, as I had regular pest control done to keep the creatures out of the house. In fact, I had not seen a spider in my home for almost two years. Seeing three separate spiders three days in a row was a big deal, but I didn't know how significant it was until I arrived in California.

As I was sitting outside the airport in Sacramento waiting for the shuttle to take me to my hotel, I looked down and there was a little brown spider sitting on my chest. That was the fourth spider in four days, and I realized there was something going on with spiders. The next day, I was sitting at the dining table at Denise's house for lunch when from the corner of my eye I saw a little movement next to my plate. It was another spider, there only for me to notice. The following day I was walking to my bedroom in her house and a large spider ran across the hallway in front of me.

After six spiders in six days, I finally decided to look up the meaning of spiders to see what message the Universe was delivering to me. What I found out resonated strongly with what was going on in my life at the time.

Spiders were a sign that my higher self was guiding me toward a deep understanding of my place and purpose in this life. They represent patience, receptivity, feminine energy, creativity, mystery, power, growth, and the shadow self. Spider is a communicator, and writers often have a spider totem. Spiders have eight eyes and eight legs, which relates to the infinity symbol and evolution. They help us tune into life's ebbs and flows, and they are the ingenious weavers of destiny.

In Native American culture, the spider represents grandmother. A couple of days after the class in California started, one of my classmates was giving me an intuitive reading. As she was talking to me, she saw a woman standing next to me that turned out to be my grandmother who had passed away a few years before. The message my grandmother wanted to share with me was she was happy I was on this new path. She indicated she had been wrong about her religious beliefs in this most recent life. My grandmother had been a Christian who believed in Heaven and Hell and was very close-minded about esoteric spirituality.

Once I acknowledged the spiders and the signs they were showing me, I stopped seeing them every day. They were there to give me a specific message, so once I received it, they didn't need to be around me anymore. About a year later, when I was writing my book, *Sacred Soul Spaces*, I had several more spider encounters in my home. They were there to show their support and to tell me to keep going on this new endeavor.

Signs are all around us. We just need to be aware of what the signs are to figure out the message they have for us. This can be an incredibly powerful tool. Before my training, I had some fear and uncertainty about my new path as a Past Life Regression Coach. The spiders and my grandmother showed me I was actually moving in a direction my higher-self resonated with and it would all be okay. Since my spider experience, I have noticed many other animal signs as well.

My suggestion to you is to pay attention to what is going on around you, and if the same animal or numbers or words keep appearing to you, it is a sign from the Universe. You may be surprised by what you find out the message is, or it may confirm what you already know.

Goddesses

Over the last few years, I have immersed myself in goddess energy and magic. I have discovered and cultivated my inner goddess, my Divine Feminine. As women, we all have the ability to call on goddess wisdom when we need it. There may be one particular goddess you resonate with and have as an ally; there may be multiple goddesses you call on. I'll share what this looks like in my world.

Several years ago a medium I was working with told me she had the strong sense of goddess energy around me. She determined the energy was the Hindu goddess Saraswati.

When I researched who she was, immediately I knew this was me. Saraswati (sometimes spelled Sarasvati) is my personal goddess.

Saraswati, or "The One Who Flows," is the Hindu goddess of knowledge, music, art, wisdom, science and higher learning. She is often depicted wearing a white sari and sitting on a white lotus, representing light, knowledge and truth. In her hands, she holds a book representing true knowledge and learning, a mala representing meditation, spirituality and inner reflection, a water pot that represents the power to separate right from wrong, and a musical instrument called a veena, which symbolizes all creative arts and sciences.

Saraswati has two birds associated with her, the most common of which is a white swan, symbolizing spiritual perfection and transcendence. The other is a peacock, which represents celebration of dance and colorful splendor. The peacock has the ability to eat snakes, so they also represent the ability to transmute the snake poison of the self into the plumage of enlightenment.

Saraswati is called upon to help manifest thoughts, dreams and passions. She invokes a flow of energy in the dreamer and artist, allowing the creative lifeforce to flow within. She inspires.

For me, Saraswati is the embodiment of who I am in this lifetime. I am a scientist by training with a doctorate degree. I have always been an artist as well. Growing up, I was a dancer and did other artistic endeavors. As an adult, I have been an interior designer for more than ten years and a jewelry designer for almost thirty years. My passion in this life is to continue learning and growing. I strive to incorporate my spirituality into my daily life through meditation and connection. My daily mantra is "Stay in the flow."

Since getting to know Saraswati so well in my life, I started exploring the power of the other goddesses. There are thousands of goddesses throughout human history from all parts of the world. Some are more famous because of oral and written stories throughout time from particular cultures, such as the rich Greek mythology stories. Each goddess represents a different aspect of the Divine Feminine. We can call in their power to aide and guide us. We can realize their nature inside of us, just waiting to be discovered.

I love using Doreen Virtue's Goddess Guidance Oracle Cards and, more recently, Colette Baron-Reid's Goddess Power Oracle Cards. When I am pulling a card of the day, I'll ask for the goddess I need guidance from that particular day to come forward. I then draw a card to see who is there. The cards don't lie.

If you specifically want to call in love to your life, here are some of the goddesses who can guide you:

Aine – Irish goddess of love, summer, wealth and sovereignty

Aphrodite – Greek goddess of passion, love, sexual energy (Venus is her Roman counterpart)

Astarte – Semitic goddess of sexual love, maternity, and fertility

Benzai-Ten – Japanese goddess of everything that flows - water, music, eloquence, knowledge, beauty, the arts, and love

Branwen – Celtic goddess of love and beauty

Freyja – Nordic goddess of love, magic, divination, fertility, celebration and passion

Frigg – Germanic goddess of marriage and women

Guinevere – Celtic goddess of true love and romance

Hathor – Egyptian goddess of love, childbirth, beauty, and music

Inanna – Sumerian goddess of sexual love, procreation, fertility and war.

Ishtar – Mesopotamian goddess of love, procreation, boundaries, nurturing, mothering, sensuality, fertility, healing, protection, war and wisdom

Isolt – Celtic goddess of relationship love

Kuan Yin – Eastern goddess of compassion, purity, nurturing love and gentle power

Lilith – Jewish goddess of independence, attracting healthy, interdependent relationships

Mary Magdalene – goddess of unconditional love, forgiveness and opening your heart to more love

Milda – Lithuanian goddess of love and freedom

Oshun – Yoruba goddess of luxury, pleasure, sexuality, fertility, beauty and love

Persephone – Greek goddess of harvest and fertility

Qetesh – Egyptian goddess of love, beauty, and sex

Radha (or Radharani) – Hindu goddess of love and worship

There are numerous ways to work with the goddesses, so have fun exploring how to do this for yourself. Access your Divine Feminine.

Angels

Working with angels is the newest of my spiritual practices. As mentioned earlier, I invoke the blue light of Archangel Michael daily to maintain my energy, keeping out energy seen and unseen. As an empath, this one method has helped me more than I could have ever imagined.

There are seven Archangels, which are described below (from Sunny Dawn Johnston's, *Invoking the Archangels*):

Archangel Chamuel – Pink energy; unconditional love and adoration; helps with career, life purpose, finding lost items, building and strengthening relationships, world peace and seeking soulmates

Archangel Gabriel – White energy; helps with communication in any area; adoption; child conception and fertility; journalism and writing

Archangel Jophiel – Golden Yellow energy; creativity, art and beauty; helps those who feel spiritually lost, depressed or in despair

Archangel Michael – Blue energy; protection, guidance and strength; helps with protection, direction, self-esteem, motivation, courage, commitment, faith, energy, vitality, life's purpose, and releasing fear

Archangel Raphael – Green energy; healing physical, mental, emotional and spiritual bodies; helps with eliminating or reducing addictions and cravings, healing on all levels, guidance and support for healers, physical and spiritual eyesight, clairvoyance, and finding lost pets

Archangel Uriel – Red energy; illuminates situations, gives prophetic information and offers transmutation; helps with insight, clarity, peace, vision, problem solving, writing, new ideas, study and tests

Archangel Zadkiel – Violet energy; forgiveness, mercy and benevolence; helps with forgiveness of self and others, emotional healing, compassion, freedom, finding lost objects, and memory

Final thought: Whether you rely solely on your own wisdom or choose to be guided by the unseen, know you have access to the information you need to make the best decisions for you. Trust your inner wisdom.

"The best and most beautiful things in this world cannot be seen or even heard, but must be felt with the heart."
— ***Helen Keller***

7

Finding Your Ideal Partner

"And then my soul saw you and it kind of went, "Oh, there you are. I've been looking all over for you."
– Unknown

Once you have gone through the experiences and techniques to heal your deep wounds and have created a life you love and thrive in, you are in a position to meet your ideal partner. It's when you truly love yourself inside and outside as a whole and healthy person that you can have clear judgment if someone is right or wrong for you. When we are injured, we tend to forgive our partner's behaviors because we are fearful we won't meet anyone better. I am here to say you *can* meet and maintain a relationship with a loving, ideal partner, despite what you have experienced in the past.

If you are currently in a relationship, you might, after having gone through the processes in this workbook, wonder whether you can stay with that person. That is for you to decide. If their behavior is not up to the standard you have set for yourself and they are unwilling to go through the process of healing themselves, it may not be in your best interest to keep them in your life. If, however, they are willing to do the work on themselves, or if you find that you, not they, were the problem, the relationship has the potential to work.

In Chapter 3, you created a list of characteristics your ideal partner would have and where you were not matched up to those characteristics at that time. I want you now to go back to the list and review the characteristics you deemed important. Do they all resonate with you? Are there any new characteristics you want to add? Are there any you want to delete? Where do you match up to those characteristics at this time? It is this list that will help you assess whether the new people you are meeting are potentials for you.

Before I get into the mechanics of the dating process I recommend, I will share with you my story of finding my perfect partner, Skip.

My Story

Once I felt like I truly knew myself again and all of my likes and dislikes, it was time to test the dating waters. My coach and I devised a plan for dating. I would put my scientist hat on and be very objective when I was meeting people. I would do my best to stay out of my emotions and be the observer of the men and of myself. In order to do the experiment, I decided to try online dating as it was my best opportunity to meet people outside of my sphere of influence. I wanted to use a service that asked a lot of questions, so I could see the answers before I would ever meet the person. I chose OK Cupid as the dating platform.

I created my profile and answered over a thousand questions in various categories. The algorithm calculated my answers with the potential matches' answers and gave a percentage match overall, as well as a percentage match for each category. I could see all of the answers given by the potential dates. I decided an 80% match or higher would yield the greatest possibility of a mate for me, so anything less was automatically disregarded.

Another strategy I used to eliminate potentials before I ever talked to them or even read their profile was to look at their eyes in the pictures they had provided. Eyes are truly the windows to the soul and can tell you a lot about a person; therefore, men who wore sunglasses in the majority of pictures, including their main profile picture, were immediately disqualified. As I looked into their eyes I would try to get a feel for any underlying emotions there. If there was anger, it would be grounds for disqualification. This narrowed the dating pool drastically; however, it also saved me a lot of time and grief.

Once the matches had passed the eye test, I read their profile to determine whether or not I wanted to move further. My coach guided me to not judge the men on their overall looks, just the eyes first and then the profile. The reason is that an amazing soulmate match may not be the hottest, sexiest person you are instantly attracted to. It may be the person you get to know over time or has a big age difference or body different from what you might think you could be with.

Once a match had passed all of these initial tests, I would then reach out to them or respond to their reaching out to me. After a few messages back and forth I would then have a phone conversation as quickly as possible so I could hear them and really communicate.

After the initial phone conversation, a date would be set. I chose to do lunch dates, so they could be cut off easily and stay in the "friend" zone without any worries. If a date wasn't going well, I had the excuse of having to get back to work. If it was going well, it would be an opportunity to set a next date.

With this experiment, I met eight guys within a three-week period. After each date, I would keep a journal of what I liked and disliked about them, as well as the experience overall. This was my way to keep track of any red flags that might be there and to really hone-in on what I wanted in a partner. As each date went on, the guys were getting better and better. I did not have any bad dates. The men who didn't make it to a second date just didn't match enough with me and what I wanted. They were all very nice, quality men.

There were two of the eight that made it to date number two and three. One of them dropped off after date number three. The other one ended up being an ongoing casual dating thing for several weeks. There were red flags that eventually came up in our time together which told me not to continue. After that experience, I took a break from online dating to date myself again. About a month and a half later, I met the person who would end up being the love of my life and is now my husband and life partner.

Meeting the Love of My Life

The day I met Skip wasn't like most days. It was the yearly Community Service Day for the local Realtors chapter, and I was volunteering to help paint over graffiti on buildings downtown. When I arrived that morning, there was a man I hadn't seen before there to paint with us. Even though I had never met him, he seemed so familiar to me, like I knew him from somewhere. This immediate reaction was strong enough that when we were splitting into teams, I consciously (or maybe subconsciously) chose to be on a team with him. It wasn't that he was just so extremely good looking, though he is very handsome; it was an innate pull towards him. We spent the morning talking about our lives.

When we met, my divorce was almost final, and his was still early in the process, though he and his ex had already been apart for a full year. They had a business together that they had to divorce as well, which had lengthened the process. He had moved down to Olympia to start a new life. The more we talked, the more intrigued I was. Our conversation just flowed, and it felt like we had known each other for a long time. After the painting, it was time to head back to the Realtor office for lunch. He decided he needed to get back to his own office, so we parted ways. I invited him to come to the other weekly real estate meetings, but I did not know if and when I would see him again.

A week or two later, he showed up at the morning real estate meeting, and my physiology immediately changed. There was an excitement in my body about seeing him. He sat across the room, but I could feel my connection to him. For the next several weeks, I only saw him at the meetings, and we weren't able to talk much.

In early July, I took my son to the annual BBQ festival in our town, put on by the Chamber of Commerce. As I was walking along, I noticed Skip working one of the chamber booths, and again, my body had an immediate reaction. I didn't go over immediately, as my son had pulled my attention away to something else. We kept walking and naturally ended up near the booth, where he noticed me. We made small talk for a short while and then my son and I continued on. A bit later, his booth shift was over and we ended up in the same area again talking to mutual friends. I invited him to my divorce party I was going to be having a couple of weeks later. I wasn't sure if he would make it, but I knew I had to try to figure out ways to be in proximity to him. He was still very new to the area and didn't know a lot of people, so I thought I could help introduce him to my friends.

He did show up to the divorce party, which excited me. He was still depressed about his divorce situation, so at that time, he was not reciprocating my interest. At the end of the party, we were talking about dancing with a couple of my friends. It turned out that like me, he loved to dance, and they invited us to come East Coast swing dancing with them sometime. We decided we could go dancing together, even if it was just as friends.

The day we had set for dancing was on the same day I had a Rotary lunch event, which went all afternoon. I ended up being a little late to dinner to meet Skip and my friends. While Skip went to the bathroom to wash his hands, my girlfriend informed me that he seemed very nervous (in a good way) to be there with us. We had a great dinner and then went to the dance location.

I had taken some swing dancing in graduate school, but Skip was brand new to it. He picked it up pretty fast, and we spent the night dancing together. I felt happy and free. I was giggling, which made him smile and giggle. It was so easy.

After dancing, we went to the bar downstairs to have a nightcap. I had no idea what would happen after that, but it had been a great night. When we were parting, he invited me to go to a networking event with him that upcoming week, so I said yes. I wanted to spend as much time with him as I could.

A few days later, I drove to his house so we could carpool to the event. We had a great time. It was hard to tell if he was liking me as a friend or something more. My intuition said it was more. When we got back to his house at the end of the night, I invited him to hang out that upcoming Saturday. His immediate reaction was to say no. He seemed fearful our hanging out would turn into more than just friendship, which he wasn't ready for. A few minutes later, I was backing out of his driveway when I saw him rushing over to my car. When I rolled my window down, he said, that yes, he did want to go out on Saturday.

On the Friday night before the "date," I was driving around town with my best friend and her wife looking for a place to eat dinner and hang out. Skip called to make plans for the next day. We decided we would go to Seattle.

The following morning, I picked Skip up at his house and we began what would be the longest, best date I have ever had. We started at the Seattle Art Museum. As we talked about art, there was a lot of standing close to each other and flirting. It had been years since I had been to an art museum, and it was so nice to be there with someone who was interested in being there with me. After the museum, we had lunch and then went to the aquarium so I could show off my knowledge of fish and marine life, then we took a ride on the Seattle Great Wheel. At this point in the day, things were getting very flirty. After the wheel, we toured the Pike Place Market and decided to head back to Olympia for dinner.

After eating at a sushi restaurant, we went into the bookstore next door, where Skip bought me a copy of *Mutant Messages Down Under* by Marlo Morgan. It was a very thoughtful gift, as I was going to Australia in a couple of months. We went back to my house and watched two movies, *What the Bleep Do We Know?!* and *The Secret*. For me, showing him those movies was a test to see how he would react to my spiritual side.

At the end of the second movie, it was well after midnight and time for me to drive him home. He talked about his conflict of liking me but not being ready to date. He had wanted to hold my hand most of the day, but held himself back. We decided to stay in the friend zone so he could continue getting over his failed marriage. Despite the conversation about being just friends, there was definitely more to our relationship, and we both knew it. We had just been on the absolute best date of my life, doing all of the things I love to do. It was fun, and it was easy.

After the date, we talked and texted daily, sometimes several times a day. We were still "just friends." My coach at the time had to continually work with me to see the longer-term vision of our relationship as I worked on my patience. We both knew he was my person. I could feel it in my body. I knew it at the deep intuitive place inside myself. I had to wait for him to see it and know it too.

A few weeks later, I invited Skip to a Labor Day party my friend was throwing at her house. He fit right into our group of friends, and we had a great time. On the way home, he talked about how he was sexually attracted to me and wanted to have an affair, but did not want a relationship yet. I held strong, saying I wanted more and was worth more than that. Similar conversations came up several more times over the next few months.

One night in the early fall, he decided to come over to make me dinner. As we ate, he told me he was thinking he possibly needed to date/sleep around to get over the divorce. At this point I was quite invested, and though it hurt to hear it I told him I would be his wing man so he could get it out of his system. After dinner we went downtown to one of the bars with local music. When we got out of the car, I reminded him I was going to be his wing man and help him find a woman.

Then, as we were crossing the street to the bar, he suddenly grabbed my hand. I told him that was not going to get him a new woman and joked about really playing the role of his wing man. We grabbed a couple of drinks and found a booth bench to sit on. Not too long after that, he turned to me and kissed me. My body tingled from head to toe. We spent the night at the bar cuddling, holding hands and kissing – everything I had been wanting.

When we got back to my house, it was really late and cold. Skip had ridden his motorcycle, so I told him he could stay over but it would not turn into sex. We both slept so well that night. The next day, he said he felt like he could breathe better.

He still wasn't ready to be in a relationship, so it didn't go any further at this point. We continued to do our daily texting and talking. On the weekends, we would hang out. We would hold hands and make out, but nothing more than that. We also planned to go to a friend's Halloween party as two eighties icons: Billy Idol and Madonna.

The day of the Halloween party, Skip came over to get ready with me. We punked out his hair, then, as I was doing his guyliner, I decided to bend down to kiss him. I wanted him to know how I felt, and not just with my words. He kissed me back with passion and love. We went to the party and had a great time. After the party, we went back to my house and started making out. We got yellow hairspray all over my teal sofa, but it was completely worth it. He asked me if I wanted him to take me upstairs. I said yes. It was our first time making love. It was a beautiful experience.

The next day, he went home, and I wasn't sure how our relationship was going to change. We talked in the evening, and he told me he still wasn't ready for a relationship. I told him I would not just be his fuck buddy and I couldn't do the pretend relationship anymore. I ended it. I told him we could no longer talk and text daily. It was just too hard on my emotions.

We had plans to go to the chamber auction the following weekend, and since we had already bought the tickets we decided we would still go together. All week leading up to the auction we did not talk or text each other. I missed him so much. It was painful, but I knew it was the right thing for me to do. I went to pick him up for the auction, and it was strained at first. He had missed me a lot too, but still wasn't ready.

One of the live auction items that night was a week at a condo in Maui. Neither of us had been to Maui, and I wanted to bid on it. Skip and I made a deal. We would bid on the condo. If we won, and he still wasn't ready for a relationship by the time the trip came around, I would just go with one of my friends. Otherwise, it was assumed that we would go as a couple. We did end up winning the bid, so there was one thing holding us together.

A week or so later, I decided I wanted to buy a house. My rental period for my house was getting ready to expire and they wanted to put the house on the market. It was not the house I wanted to buy, but I found one in the same neighborhood in my price point that had a lot of potential. I asked Skip to do my mortgage for me. My agent wrote up the offer, and we were on a new journey.

I wanted Skip to do the mortgage because I trusted him implicitly, and I wanted to have regular contact with him again. Over the month of working with him on the mortgage, we grew close again. I had my birthday party a week or two before Christmas. Skip ended up staying the night.

My house closed the day after Christmas, and I had only a week to paint the house and move in before my lease at the other house ended. Skip, along with some of my amazing friends, volunteered to help me paint the rooms. Each day he showed up to help me get the house ready. One night, near the end of the painting, we were in the kitchen. He grabbed me and kissed me. For the next several days, we would regularly kiss and hold hands. Thanks to him and the rest of my faithful crew, I was all moved in before New Year's.

On New Year's Day, Skip flew down to Arizona with a group of his friends to watch the Seahawks/Cardinals football game. When he landed, he called me with some shocking news: he had told his friends we were officially dating. This was a huge step in our relationship, as we had not said that to each other at that point. This is what I had been wanting for months. I was so excited I couldn't wait until he got back to town, and I knew he felt the same.

It had taken seven months from the time we met for our dating to become official. One of the traits I wanted in my mate was patience, and I originally was not matched there.

This was my first lesson in patience with Skip.

Once we started officially dating, we began a new chapter in my patience journey. It took a year and three months of dating in this capacity before he was ready to move into my house. It took another year and a half for him to change his mind about never wanting to get married again.

At this point, you might be wondering why I endured the emotional roller coaster ride with Skip, after all I had been through in my other relationships and the work I had been doing on healing myself.

Looking back, I would not have been able to get through all of it without the wise counsel of my coach at the time. He had me keep checking in with myself about how I was feeling, despite what Skip might be saying at the time. He had me look at ten years in the future to see if Skip was still there and, if so, whether I was happy. My coach was psychic, so he was getting his own information from his guides about the relationship with Skip. Everything pointed to yes, Skip was my person.

I had a few friends who advised me to let it go, that he just wasn't into me in that way. They thought he would need to date around for a long time. I knew intuitively it was not the case, so I had to filter out their comments and thoughts. I had to look and feel past the verbal information Skip was feeding me about not wanting a relationship and instead look at his actions. He actually did want a relationship, and we were in one that entire time. He had so much fear of getting hurt again. I had to show him time and again I was not going to hurt him.

Those first seven months were all about building our friendship, and over time, he became my best friend. I was able to be myself with him, and he was able to be himself with me. I let him be vulnerable. He cried on my shoulder time and time again. He needed to heal, and I gave him the space to do so, as best as I could without losing contact.

After Halloween, when I "broke up" with him, it really was what both of us needed to be able to see the relationship for what it was and give us space to see what we needed and wanted. Of course there was a chance it was really over, and I had to know for myself that I would be okay no matter what happened with us. I had to be true to myself.

From Skip's side, he had gotten out of a twenty-five-year relationship. The divorce was a shock to his system. He had wanted to be the couple married for their entire lives. The dream overrode his realization that his relationship was not as great as it once had been. He's loyal and he probably would have stayed the course for many more years.

When I met him, he was in a dark place; he thought he wanted to be a miserable old man who lived alone with a dog and never found love again. He was angry with his ex for changing their life together. The night we went dancing was the first time he knew someone else could be attracted to him. My smiling and giggling had sparked a newfound interest in life.

During all of those months of hanging out, he was living in fear of having his heart broken again. He thought it would be easier if he just kept his heart protected by not being in a relationship. Yet just as I couldn't get enough of him, he couldn't get enough of me either. The connection we had was too strong.

When I asked him what finally pushed him over the edge to tell his friends we were officially dating, he said it was out of fear of losing me. He didn't want me to think he would do something stupid in Arizona to jeopardize our relationship, and he was fearful if he didn't take the leap, I would get tired of the game and find someone else.

Fear does funny things to people. Sometimes it holds us back from doing what we really want. Other times it makes us do things we might not do otherwise because the alternative would be worse. Skip's fear had to be worked through. I was the person able to hold space for him to move through it and prompt him occasionally to make shifts in his thinking. It was not my job to fix him, and I didn't try. It was his job to work through his emotions to come out on the other side to find love again.

I share this because I want you to understand the difference between holding onto to something, like a potential relationship, out of fear versus staying true to yourself while developing a relationship that may or may not go anywhere. During those first seven months, I was continually working on myself. I took a two-week trip to Australia by myself. My goal was to be able to know at the end of the trip that I would be okay if I remained single for the rest of my life.

That seven-month roller coaster ride was not easy, but it was worth the time and effort it took to develop our friendship, which led to a serious relationship and ultimately to marriage. As I previously mentioned, it was a three-year journey once we were in an official relationship to get married. I knew Skip was my person. He knew I was his person. He didn't think he ever wanted or needed to be married again. The legal binding had not guaranteed the success of his first marriage, so why would it for any other relationship?

I on the other hand knew I would like to be married again. The most important aspect of this for me was the spiritual side. I didn't need a marriage certificate. What I did want and need was a verbal commitment and ceremony expressing my love and devotion. What

I learned along the way was I needed to neutralize my emotions around the experience and expectation. The more thought and emotion I put into it, the farther away it seemed. By neutralizing the emotions, I became okay with whatever the outcome might be. If we got married, great. If we didn't get married, great. It was when I finally released the outcome one way or another that it happened.

When we finally decided to get married, it was truly about us and our relationship, nothing else. We planned to get married in Thailand during our vacation to celebrate my birthday. Though I had less than a month to prepare, everything fell into place beautifully. I found the perfect dress easily, and no alterations were needed. We found a beautiful ring for me. We told friends and family just a week or two before we left on the trip, explaining we just wanted a simple ceremony for the two of us, and we would have a party when we got back.

The trip to Thailand was magical. We stayed in four locations within the country. The hotels were given advanced notice that we were on our honeymoon, so they had each room prepared with love swans and flowers when we arrived. The wedding ceremony was on the second to last day in the country, when we were down south at a resort across from the beach. We read our personally written vows to each other as our tour guide photographed the ceremony. My long-term dream of marrying the love of my life had come true.

Past Lives and Energy

Since becoming a certified Past Life Regression coach, I have had the opportunity to delve into some of my past lives with Skip to see how our relationship dynamics played out in other realities. I had an intuitive knowing that we had been together before, possibly many times, based on that feeling, from the very first time we met, that I knew him.

The most detailed life I have viewed of us was a Native American life in the Great Plains of America. I was the husband, and Skip was my loving, supportive wife. My daughter in this life was our son in that life. My mother was our granddaughter, which resonates strongly with how our relationship is in this life. Skip is extremely supportive of me and my endeavors and has been since day one of our friendship. He and my daughter got along from the beginning of their relationship, and he has become her significant male role model in this life.

Sometimes I have random memories pop into my mind of other lives we have shared. In one life, he was a king and I was his favorite concubine. In another, we were a black couple, fighting for civil rights in the 1960s. The common themes throughout these lives has been of love and respect. I often joke because of how often we have come together in different lives, we tried to make it as challenging as possible to find each other in this life. It took us more than forty years to find each other this time around.

I can feel Skip's energy in a way I have never felt before. Being an empath, I can feel people generally, but the connection we have makes the feeling even more intense. There was one time when we were sitting on the couch and I got an overwhelming feeling of heaviness in my chest. I knew it wasn't me, so I described the sensation to him and asked if that was how he was feeling at that moment, and it was. Another time we were driving on the freeway past his old house with his ex-wife. All of a sudden, my body started producing tears and I got really sad. Again, I knew it wasn't me. I told him what was going on and he confirmed he was feeling sad at that moment about the loss of his marriage.

Skip is also my perfect complement. When I am anxious or stressed, he has the ability to calm me down. He reenergizes me. I can actually feel our energetic connection when we touch. Sometimes when we are laying in bed, holding each other with our heads and feet touching, there is a circular movement of energy moving through our bodies. This is something I have never experienced before.

When we make love, the emotions and physical sensations are more intense than I have ever felt. Our energy together is exponential. We are in sync. Our bodies merge together as one. There are even times where I can feel what is going on in his body inside of my own body when I touch him. This is a love beyond what I have known in this life.

Meeting and Dating New People

Before you even consider dating, I really want you to go through the self-assessments and work on yourself to heal those parts of you that are injured. If you skip this step, you will likely end up right back where you started in a less-than-stellar relationship or attracting the same kind of people you do not want to be in a relationship with. I see this often with my friends and acquaintances who think they have healed and love themselves. It is very clear to outside observers that this is not the case.

For some of you, meeting new people and dating is a fun process. Others of you might be dreading the dating game. I want to help you make it as easy, fun and successful as possible. In this section, I discuss the strategies I used when I was ready to date after my divorce.

Keep in mind each person is different in how they are designed. Some are meant to do "cold calling," like doing online dating. Others will find success meeting someone from their network of friends. It's great to step outside of your comfort zone. It is also important to stay true to who you are.

One of the most important things in the early stages of dating is to keep emotions out of the equation. This can be harder than said, as we are all emotional creatures by nature. What I'm asking you to do is to be an analytical observer for the interactions leading up to and through the first date with someone. Pretend to be a scientist collecting data.

Organic vs. Non-organic

Organic

You may be fortunate enough to live in an area with an abundance of people you can meet organically. When you are participating in new activities or going out with your friends, it provides opportunities to meet people naturally. Your friends and family may also be sources of dating potentials. Let them know you are ready to date. Be clear about what you are looking for in a perfect mate so they can prescreen for you.

Getting out of your normal routine will help to put you in the path of new people to meet. You can try business mixers if you are a businessperson. You can try speed dating if they have it in your area. There are numerous Meetup groups based on specific interests you could participate in to meet new people. Consider taking a short class that would attract a mixture of men and women. You don't want all of your activities to be same sex, unless that is what you are attracted to.

The most important thing is to put yourself out into the world. You will not meet new people if you stay home. You will not likely meet new people if you continue to go to the same places all of the time with your friends and family. Be out in the world living and exploring. Don't be afraid to strike up a conversation with someone new, even at the grocery store, at one of your kids' activities, etc.

When you meet someone naturally, check in with yourself to see what initially attracted you to them. Can they hold a conversation? I want you to look into their eyes and try to read them. See if there is anything that stands out to you. Notice how your body feels and try to override what your mind is thinking. Meet them at the soul level, not just the physical level. You may not know why you are interested in talking to them at first, and that is okay.

You may want to ask a couple of probing questions that will tell you immediately if it is worth continuing the conversation with them. You can figure out ahead of time what one or two major deal-breakers would be and determine if they pass the test. If they don't, you haven't invested much time and energy and should be able to move on easily. It's better to know sooner than later if there is something that will prevent the relationship from working out long-term.

For example, one of my deal-breakers is cigarette smoking. If the person is a smoker, I know it will not work with the lifestyle I choose. Another deal-breaker for me is if they are dogmatically religious. I am very spiritual, and I know a partnership will not work with someone whose fundamental belief system is at odds with my own.

Non-organic

Even if you have a plethora of organic dating opportunities, consider expanding your pool of potentials with online dating. There are sites you can use for free, although I prefer sites that require a small financial investment. This allows you to be more discreet about your searches, protecting your identity until you want to be known. A little monetary skin in the game tends to make people a little more serious about the dating process.

A few of the online dating sites have extensive questionnaires which help to match you up with like-minded people. I am a fan of this because you want to have some basic things in common if your relationship is going to work. I particularly enjoyed the site OK Cupid because I could see every answer of the person I was checking out. When I used this site, my rule of thumb was to only consider people that were an 80% match or higher, as I mentioned earlier. Pick one or two sites that fit you and your personality.

When creating an online profile, you want to be very careful about representing who you are and what you want to attract. The words and pictures you use are your marketing tools and can work for you or against you. Have friends and family read your profile to make sure it represents you authentically.

Once you have access to potential dates on a site, it is time to put your scientist hat on. Before you read any specific profiles or judge looks (good or bad), I want you first to look at the eyes of the person. Notice if you see any anger or sadness. Is there anything that stands out to you, immediately giving you concern? Underlying anger is not permissible in my world, so I recommend moving on if there are signs of anger. Sadness is usually something that can be healed with time. If the main profile picture shows the person wearing sunglasses, move on. They do not want to be seen for who they are.

I want you to do your best to not let someone's look determine your interest level or lack thereof. Sometimes our perfect match comes in a package that looks different than what we normally are attracted to. The point is to give someone you might not otherwise go on a date with a chance. Looks fade with age. The intellect and the soul do not.

Once the person has passed the initial eyes test, it is time to read the profile. Notice any wording that concerns you. You want to narrow the dating pool down by weeding out anyone that raises red flags. Trust your instinct. It will not fail you.

When you have narrowed down your choices, you can start communication. In my experience, having a phone conversation is good start because you will be able to get a sense of how they communicate. Texting and messaging are okay to make the very initial contact, but it is too hard to read tone and context with written dialogue. If the conversation goes well, suggest an in-person meeting if they don't do so first.

When setting up a first date, I recommend only doing a daytime date, such as coffee or lunch. This limits the amount of time you have to spend with your date, and it gives you an easy out if you are not enjoying yourself. It also takes away the possibility of drinking, which can change behavior, lower inhibitions and remove your better judgment. You want your mind to be clear in the early stages so you can properly assess what you are liking and not liking about the person and the experience. If the first date is going well, you can always make a plan for a second date.

After each new person you meet, document your likes and dislikes. You can use a journal or, if you prefer, an Excel spreadsheet. At the top, write the person's name. In the first column, write all of the things you like about the person and have enjoyed with the experience of going out with them. In the second column, write down all the things you don't like about the person or about the situation. Be objective. Once you have met a few people and you have your lists of likes and dislikes, you will begin to see trends and be able to compare among them. There might be things that become an instant no for you, and if so, you can cut your losses early.

Name of Person	
Likes	*Dislikes*

I highly recommend waiting to have sex with the potential partner until you have had at least three dates. Sex complicates emotions, and if the sex is good it can make you lose your better judgment.

Once you have gotten to know someone better, you can compare your list of likes to the list you previously created of the characteristics of your perfect mate. When I did this for each potential, it became clear where they were lacking. When I met and got to know my current husband and examined my perfect mate characteristics, he had every single characteristic on my list.

Letting Go of the Outcome

"The way to love anything is to realize that it may be lost."
— Gilbert K. Chesterton

One of the things I had to learn along the way in my process of finding and keeping my ideal partner was I had to let go of the outcome of any particular relationship. Even if I wanted something to work out with a specific person, I could not control it. This was difficult at times, given that I am a recovering control freak, conditioned from so many years of living in fear of not being loved.

I had to put my trust in the Universe that whatever was meant to happen would happen, and I would be okay no matter what. I had to take the emotion out of my desire to have a relationship, so it could flow naturally into my life.

I recommend you do whatever you can to not put all of your eggs in one basket until you are ready to take a relationship to the next level. You may start out dating a few guys. At some point, there will be one that stands out to you. When you choose to be monogamous you will still need to let go of the outcome. This is your opportunity to get to know them at all levels. Maintain a position for yourself that you can leave the relationship at any time and be okay emotionally and financially.

I do not recommend moving in with someone until you know them very well. Once you move in, there are more expectations that can easily be put on the relationship, and it is harder to get out quickly if you need to. If they show you a part of themselves you don't like so much before you move in, know and trust it is not going to get better. In fact, it is likely to get worse when they will feel more comfortable being themselves.

If after a period of time there are no red flags and you mutually agree to move in, stay in the place of curiosity with your partner to keep assessing if this is a good match for you. Keep letting go of the outcome to take it to the next level of marriage if that is your ultimate goal in the relationship.

If it is meant to be, it will happen. Even though I had healed myself in so many areas of my life, I am still human. I had to continually work on letting go of the outcome of being married to Skip. He had to get to the place in his mind where he was ready, which was on a different timeline than mine. I had to be patient. I had to be okay with never getting married to him. I knew he was my person and we were going to be together.

If you really want marriage and your partner does not, take a look at why it is so important for you to have the marriage certificate. What does marriage mean to you? Will it change the relationship? Will it change who you are together? You may decide that it is so important that you need to find a different partner who is willing to get married. Or you may discover marriage is not as important as you have made it out to be and you will be okay if you never get married. Both are okay. This is your life and your relationship.

Final thought: Have fun and be open to the dating experience. It will all be worth it! Be neutral and let go of the outcome.

"We're all a little weird. And life is a little weird. And when we find someone whose weirdness is compatible with ours, we join up with them and fall into mutually satisfying weirdness—and call it love—true love."
— **Robert Fulghum,** <u>*True Love*</u>

8

Cultivating the Relationship with Your Ideal Partner

"It is not a lack of love, but a lack of friendship that makes unhappy marriages."
— **Friedrich Nietzsche**

When you meet and fall in love with your ideal partner, it does not mean the work is over. You will continue to work on yourself and the relationship to maintain and grow. As humans, we are not static in who we are. We go through life changes and experiences that can change who we are and who we think we are. Cultivating your relationship on a daily basis will lead to a beautiful future.

In this chapter, I focus on the areas important in my relationship with my husband. I have had to learn these from failures of past relationships and learning new ideas and implementing them. While most of the topics will seem obvious, it's easy to forget how important they are. We sometimes need to be reminded to make them a part of our regular routine and lifestyle.

Communication

Good communication is one of the most important things that can maintain a healthy relationship with your partner. This means you talk about the good things, and even more importantly, you talk about the bad and hard things in life. Whether your sharing is personal to you or about you as a couple, or the greater world you live in, having open, honest communication will bring you closer together.

Your partner cannot read your mind. Even if they have developed their psychic ability and might know when something is off, it is up to you to bring up any concerns or issues you might be having. Do not expect them to know what is going on because of the behavior you are exhibiting. That is unfair to your partner, who might be going through some things of their own at the same time. You need to verbalize your thoughts and feelings. This will help them to verbalize theirs as well.

If you need to discuss something that is challenging for you, think about what you are going to say first before you blurt something out you don't intend. If you approach a tough conversation with emotion, you are likely to be met with equal or more emotion. If you can objectively speak what you need to without the emotion and without blame, you are more likely to be heard and understood.

All couples have various strategies that will work best in their relationship, so there is not a one size fits all recommendation that I have for you. The one thing that all couples can and should do when communicating about more challenging ideas is to try to understand where the other partner is coming from. Sometimes it might be personal. Other times it might be them projecting something onto the other person. Whatever it is, truly listen to them.

Give your partner a safe space to share all they need to without responding until they are completely finished with their thoughts. If you interrupt them in the middle of a thought, you are not really listening to what they are saying fully and may misinterpret their intent. This can be hard to do, particularly if you feel like they are blaming or attacking you about something. Do your best to remain calm. Once they have finished, you can have the opportunity to respond to what they are saying and ask any clarifying questions you might need to understand their position better. It's always a good idea to repeat back to them a summary of what you heard them say to make sure you heard them correctly.

It is okay to listen to what they say and take a break from the conversation if needed.

The break might need to be a few minutes up to a few hours. Try not to go more than a day without addressing the issue. Beyond this time, the issue can get neglected and the other person left feeling like their thoughts are not important.

Do you want to be right or do you want to be happy? Learn when to share concerns. If you nit-pick over every little thing, it will wear your partner down and they will begin to think they can't do anything right. Think about how important it really is. Some issues are going to be very important to address. Others, not so much.

If you have several issues you want to bring to your partner, focus on only one at a time in a conversation, unless they are intricately connected. You don't want to overwhelm your partner and you don't want to dilute your message. This is known as fair fighting, researched and written about extensively by Dr. John Gottman of the Gottman Institute.

If your partner is bringing something to you, don't respond by throwing something negative back at them. This will only make matters worse. You can bring it up at a separate time when things are calm again.

When you have an issue to bring to your partner, come from a place of feeling rather than blaming. For instance, if my partner does something I judge as inappropriate or don't like, I might say, "The thing you did makes me feel sad, embarrassed, hurt…" etcetera, rather than, "You are wrong for doing that." How we phrase our words has a huge impact on how our words are received. Feelings cannot be argued with. Statements that come off as fact or blaming can be argued with.

Create space daily, if possible, to connect with your partner and communicate about anything that may have happened that particular day, whether it was great or not so great. Ask them how their day was. Share how your day was. The more you can communicate on a regular basis, the less likely you will have major difficult conversations. You will be able to discuss things as they come up in the moment rather than letting them build up. It will help you place the "blame" where it truly lies instead of projecting the blame onto the other person when it doesn't belong there.

My husband and I communicate a couple of times throughout the day via text and then we talk about our days at night when we are home together. We will send each other sweet texts, just to remind each other how much we love each other, are thinking about each other and are grateful for each other. When possible, we have a sit-down dinner with each other, and if the kids are home, with them as well. This is our opportunity to talk about the day. It brings us closer together to know we are a family unit on the same page. This is one of my favorite times with my family. We also take morning walks when the schedule allows, which gives us quality, uninterrupted time with each other.

Friendship

Before my husband and I were dating officially, we were friends first for several months. This friendship was one of the important things in my life, and it is to this day. We tend to give our friends a lot of leeway in accepting them and their differences from us. With our love partners, we have a tendency to forget they are their own separate person from us with their own journey. We may not always like the journey, but we can be there to support them on the journey. As my friend, I want the best for him, regardless of how it relates to me.

When I get frustrated by something my partner says or does, or if we are having a disagreement about something, I try to remember that he is first and foremost my friend. This keeps me present with him and reminds me we are on the same team.

Respect and Trust

> *"I'll never ask you to change for me because you are perfect just the way you are."*
> **– Unknown**

Respecting and trusting our partners is one of the greatest gifts we can give to them. In my previous toxic relationships, my partners did not respect me the way I thought I should be respected. I did not trust them that they were not going to hurt me or break my heart.

With my current husband, we mutually respect each other in all areas of our lives. I respect his ideas about different things. Even if we don't always agree on a topic, I respect his ideas and decisions. He has such a huge heart, and he is always helping me to open my heart wider as well.

Although my husband did not have kids of his own, he often has good advice for me as I am parenting my children. It's because of the respect I have for him that I listen to his ideas. He often thinks about situations differently than I do from his observer position, which helps me get out of my unconscious patterns.

I trust my partner to make good decisions for himself and for us as a team. I trust him to do the right thing in his business, with his friends, with his life. I trust him with my heart, and he trusts me with his heart, most importantly.

When we respect and trust our partner to have our best interests in mind for the relationship, there is no need to be jealous of people or situations. Regardless of what someone else may do or say, our partner has the ability to say no or act in such a manner that negates the behavior of the other person. This takes worthiness and inner security on our part, and if we are healed and whole as a person, it will come naturally.

Be Whole and Healthy – Maintain Yourself Continually

Some of us have a tendency to lose ourselves in a romantic relationship. I used to do that in my previous relationships, mostly because I was trying to fill an empty hole within myself. Now that I am whole again, I make the effort to keep doing what I need to do to maintain my wholeness.

I participate in activities and groups that fill me up spiritually. I spend quality time with my tribe of girlfriends. I have time alone with myself and my thoughts. I travel alone and with my friends when I'm not travelling with my husband. I make sure I am taking care of myself so I have enough energy to take care of my husband and kids.

My husband has his own activities he does that keeps him whole and healthy. He is a runner (I am not), so he has a few running clubs he participates in. He runs half marathons with his running club friends. He volunteers on a board for a non-profit in our local community. He spends time working on his motorcycle and the car he is rebuilding. He loves to ski, snow shoe and climb mountains with his outdoorsy friends.

The point here is we each have interests we do without each other. We do not expect the other person to be there 24/7 participating in every activity we do. We support each other's independence and come together in shared activities when the time is right. When we can come together as whole people, our love and potential expand. Our lives are richer.

Be Active with Each Other

In addition to having part of our lives independent from each other, it is also important to have regular activities we share as a couple and as a family. There are some couples I know that have no common interests and spend most of their lives apart. This is not healthy from my perspective and those relationships don't usually last, unless there is mutual agreement that the relationship is okay that way.

The first date my husband and I went on was a double date with friends who love to swing dance. After the first night of dancing together, it was obvious to both of us we made good dance partners. We ended up taking group and private dance lessons for a few months.

Another activity we do together, with or without the kids and friends, is to kayak on the lake or in Puget Sound near our home. We love being on the water together. Even though we are in individual kayaks, it gives us a chance to enjoy our beautiful environment and have easy, relaxed conversation.

When the weather allows, we take morning walks around our neighborhood to get the day started. This is one of my favorite activities because it gives us quality time with each other; we are able to hold hands and talk about anything going on in our lives. It brings us closer together, and it is good for our health.

We both love to travel and explore new places, so when we have time we take short weekend trips nearby as well as longer trips out of the country. We plan for one major trip each year. So far we've been to Maui, Cancun and Thailand. We are going to Belize soon and are planning another trip to southeast Asia. When we travel, we love doing adventurous activities. We've been snorkeling, zip lining, swimming with whale sharks, jungle trekking and on our trip to Thailand, we got to feed and bathe elephants. We tour temples and ruins, we shop, we eat. We have fun together.

Before my husband, I was not a fan of motorcycles, mostly out of fear. Now I love taking motorcycle rides in the country, wrapping my arms tightly around his waist. He has helped me expand my interests.

Intimacy

Let's talk about sex, baby! Actually, intimacy is more than just sexual intercourse. It happens when we allow ourselves to be vulnerable with our partner, sharing our inner most thoughts. It can be the moments when we are looking deep into our partner's eyes to see their soul, the essence of who they truly are.

Physical touch is certainly an aspect of intimacy. It can be as simple as holding hands when sitting or walking together, or passionate love making. However you and your partner enjoy intimacy with each other, it is important to make it a natural and regular part of your life.

In my first two marriages, intimacy was lacking most of the time. With my first marriage, I didn't want to be intimate most days because I was not feeling the love. With my second marriage, after the baby was born, there were several periods in the relationship where there was no physical touch for up to six months at a time. Often the communication was lacking as well, which contributed to the lack of intimacy. I find communication and intimacy to go hand in hand. When we feel heard and seen by our partners, we feel closer to them. In most cases this naturally leads to physical intimacy.

Even if sex is not an important part of your relationship with your partner, having other types of intimacy is important. If this is not natural in your current relationship or a part of your schedule, I recommend that you actively schedule intimate time with your partner, daily if possible. This could be as simple as going to bed together at the same time and holding each other before you fall asleep. It could be snuggling on the couch in the evening after dinner. You might go out (or stay in) for a romantic dinner where you can look each other in the eyes and share deep conversation. The key is to connect with your partner beyond the day to day routine of wake up, go to work, come home and go to bed.

Planting a seed of intimacy is a great way to build the excitement and anticipation of being together. You might send a flirty text during the day alluding to that night. You might put a note in your partner's pocket for them to find that day. You could give your partner a special kiss in the morning before you go to work that suggests intimacy later that day or night. This is a conscious effort and well worth the thought and energy.

Love languages

Several years ago, I was introduced to Gary Chapman's, *The Five Love Languages*. Before that, I had no idea there could be so many ways to give and receive love and that everyone has their own way of really feeling love. This can help explain why some relationships work well and others don't. If we don't understand how we receive love, we may never fully feel it. If we don't know how our partner receives love, they may never feel it from us.

When you are in a new relationship or are just discovering this concept of love languages, it is important to identify what your personal top one or two languages are so you can share this information with your partner. Likewise, have your partner identify their top two languages. This doesn't mean all languages are not important to an individual, but they generally are not all equal. This is where respect and good communication come into play. When we are able to verbalize how we operate and hear how our partner operates, we have the ability to give and receive love in the way that it will be the most effective.

Here's a quick summary of the five love languages:

Words of affirmation – using words to build up the other person.

Examples: "You are special," "You look beautiful/handsome," "You are wise"

Gifts – giving physical gifts/presents, whether purchased or not.

Examples: bringing flowers, buying jewelry or other gifts to show love

Acts of Service – doing something for your partner that you know they would like.

Examples: making dinner/breakfast, washing dishes, mowing the yard, washing the car

Quality time – giving your partner your undivided attention for an unspecified amount of time.

Examples: taking a walk together, sitting at the dinner table talking and listening with no phone or TV distraction

Physical touch – giving any kind of physical touch to your partner.

Examples: holding hands, hugging, cuddling, kissing, sexual intercourse

If you are not sure what your top two languages are, there are quizzes you can take online for this. You may be able to figure it out right away based on the descriptions above.

When I did this myself, I was surprised to discover acts of service is my top language for receiving love, with quality time and words of affirmation closely behind. Service helps me feel like I am worthy of love if my partner is doing something for me to make my life easier. My least important language is receiving gifts. When I took a look at this, I realized my mother's way of giving love is by giving gifts. She does this for my children as well. I was not surprised to realize that is one of the reasons I did not feel like I was getting love as a child. She wasn't speaking my language.

One thing to note is the way you receive love is not always the same as the way you express love. For instance, your receiving language might be physical touch, but your giving language could be words of affirmation. There is a possibility you will need to retrain yourself on giving love to your partner the way they will receive it the best. It is worth doing this for long-term happiness and enjoyment in your relationship.

List here in order of importance your love languages:

1. _____

2. _____

3. _____

4. _____

5. _____

List here in order of importance your partner's love languages:

1. _____

2. _____

3. _____

4. _____

5. _____

Look at how they match up or contrast. Do you need to change how you give your love to your partner so they receive it from you? Do they need to change the way they give love for you to receive it?

"Marital Bliss"

I include this last section to explain what I think of when I say "Marital Bliss." Marriage, whether it is a legally binding agreement, a spiritual agreement or just a verbal agreement to be with each other, will have its ups and downs. It is all about compromise. It is about all of the things I've talked about so far in this chapter.

There will be good days and bad days, fun times and hard times. The thing to remember is to be as present in the moment as you can. Don't live in the past, bringing up things that have already been done and dealt with. Don't live in the future, where you have expectations which may not be met as the time comes. Be present. Be in the now. Be with your partner, knowing why you are together and loving each other.

When I interviewed long-term couples regarding how they maintain their marital bliss over so many years, similar answers emerged. Communication was the most important thing to a happy, long-term relationship.

In Chinese feng shui, Marital Bliss is symbolized by the union of the dragon and the phoenix. The dragon represents yang, or male energy, creativity and ambition. The phoenix represents yin, or female energy, warmth and wisdom. When they come together, they form a perfect balance of energy, symbolizing harmony, togetherness, everlasting love and successful Marital Bliss.

Final thought: Loving yourself unconditionally allows you to receive unconditional love from others. No one is perfect, but you can love them in all of their imperfections. Cultivate your love relationship to grow and thrive.

"You may not be her first, her last, or her only.
She loved before she may love again.
But if she loves you now, what else matters?
She's not perfect—you aren't either,
and the two of you may never be perfect together
but if she can make you laugh,
cause you to think twice, and admit to being human
and making mistakes, hold onto
her and give her the most you can.
She may not be thinking about you every second
of the day, but she will give you a part of her
that she knows you can break—her heart.
So don't hurt her, don't change her, don't analyze
and don't expect more than she can give.
Smile when she makes you happy, let her know
when she makes you mad, and miss her
when she's not there."
— Bob Marley

Conclusion

"The most important thing in life is to learn how to give out love, and to let it come in."
— **Morrie Schwartz**

*T*hank you for taking this journey with me through this workbook. We have covered a lot of ground. My hope for you is you work through the exercises to reveal and heal your blockages and limitations. You can create a life you love, including cultivating your own Sacred Soul Love. Sacred Soul Love begins with loving yourself, first and foremost. When you know your worth and inner beauty it is easy to see when others don't treat you in the way you deserve.

The deeper you are willing to go into examining the patterns and belief systems of yourself, your parents and your ancestral bloodline, the more likely you are to get to the root cause of any unhappiness and relationship trauma you may have in your life. You may want to interview your family to uncover even more information about the ancestral blood-line, so you can be as thorough in your clearing as possible.

The more observant and honest you can be about the negative messages you give to yourself and receive from others, the better you will be able to change those thought patterns. There is no healing without first exposing what needs to be healed. This will be an ongoing process.

Once you reveal your innermost beliefs, you have the opportunity to choose whether or not you want to make changes in your life. You have the power. The exercises and methods will help you to rewire your brain when you do them intentionally. Be patient with yourself through this process. Don't give up on yourself. Consider having trusted friends and family help you with this process to keep you accountable.

You are worthy of self-love. When you come from the place of knowing you're loved, your world changes. The way you see life changes. You begin to attract love into your world, including romantic love, if that is what you desire. Become the most important person in your life.

Environment is stronger than willpower. Do what you need to do to create physical, emotional and spiritual environments that will support the new you. Don't be afraid to let go of toxic people and situations in your life. Create a sanctuary in your home where you can immerse yourself in love and healing.

You have access to information you need to live your best life. Learn to hear and trust your inner wisdom when making decisions. Ask for help and guidance from your unseen messengers, guides and angels when you need it. You've got this!

Be patient when it comes to meeting your ideal partner. Often we get caught up in our initial emotions and think someone is "the one" without enough evidence to support it. Take time to get to know people. Understand that no one is perfect. However, if red flags come up, I don't want you to ignore them or turn them green. Trust yourself and the Universe to bring you your ideal partner. It will happen if you are intentional in your life. Have fun with the experience, and let go of the outcome.

When you meet your ideal partner, take the time and effort to cultivate your relationship. Don't become lazy. Communicate, communicate, communicate! Make time for intimacy, whatever that looks like to you and your partner. You deserve to have your own "Marital Bliss."

"Love grows by giving. The love we give away
is the only love we keep.
The only way to retain love is to give it away."
– Elbert Hubbard

Bibliography

Andrews, Ted. *Animal Speak*. Minnesota: Llewellyn Publications. 1993.

Baron-Reid, Colette. *Goddess Power Oracle: Deck and Guidebook*. California: Hay House, Inc. 2019.

Beattie, Melody. *Codependent No More: How to Stop Controlling Others and Start Caring For Yourself*. Minnesota: Hazelden Foundation. 1986.

Birren, Faber. *Color Psychology and Color Therapy: A Factual Study of the Influence of Color on Human Life*. Montana: Kessinger Publishing. 1961.

Braden, Gregg. *The Spontaneous Healing of Belief: Shattering the Paradigm of False Limits*. California: Hay House, Inc. 2008.

Bunnell, Lynda and Ra Uru Hu. *The Definitive Book of Human Design: The Science of Differentiation*. California: HDC Publishing. 2017.

Chapman, Gary. *The Five Love Languages: The Secret to Love That Lasts*. Illinois: Northfield Publishing. 2004.

Chauran, Alexandra. *Clearing Clutter: Physical, Mental and Spiritual*. Minnesota: Llewellyn Publications. 2015.

Dispenza, Dr. Joe. *You are the Placebo: Making Your Mind Matter*. California: Hay House, Inc. 2014.

Farmer, Dr. Steven. *Pocket Guide to Spirit Animals*. California: Hay House, Inc. 2012.

Giliam, James and David Unruh. "The Effects of Baker-Miller Pink on Biological, Physical and Cognitive Behaviour." *Journal of Orthomolecular Medicine* 3.4 (1988): 202-206.

Gottman, John. *The Seven Principles for Making Marriage Work*. New York: Harmony Books. 1999.

Hay, Louise. *You Can Heal Your Life*. California: Hay House, Inc. 1984.

Hay, Louise. *Mirror Work: 21 Days to Heal Your Life*. California: Hay House, Inc. 2016.

Johnston, Sunny Dawn. *Invoking the Archangels: A Nine-step Process to Heal Your Body, Mind and Soul*. Hierophant Publishing. 2012.

Kondo, Marie. *The Life-Changing Magic of Tidying Up: The Japanese Art of Decluttering and Organizing*. California: Ten Speed Press. 2014

Kwallek, Nancy, Kokyung Soon and Carol M. Lewis. "Work week productivity, visual complexity, and individual environmental sensitivity in three offices of different color interiors." *Color Research & Application* 32. 130 (2007) - 143. 10.1002/col.20298.

Linn, Denise. *Past Lives, Present Miracles*. California: Hay House, Inc. 1997.

Linn, Denise. *Soul Coaching: 28 Days to Discover Your Authentic Self*. California: Hay House, Inc. 2011.

Lipton, Dr. Bruce. *The Biology of Belief: Unleashing the Power of Consciousness, Matter, and Miracles*. California: Hay House, Inc. 2005.

Mohagheghzadeh A., P. Faridi, M. Shams-Ardakani, and Y. Ghasemi. "Medicinal Smokes." *J Ethnopharmacol*. 108.2 (2006):161-84.

Morgan, Marlo. *Mutant Message Down Under*. New York: HarperCollins. 1991.

Ortner, Nick. *The Tapping Solution: A Revolutionary System for Stress-Free Living*. California: Hay House, Inc. 2013.

Parkyn, Chetan. *Human Design: Discover the Person You Were Born to Be*. California: New World Library. 2009.

Segal, Inna. *The Secret Language of Your Body: The Essential Guide to Health and Wellness*. New York: Atria Paperback. 2010.

Tchi, Rodika. *The Healing Power of Smudging: Cleansing Rituals to Purify Your Home, Attract Positive Energy and Bring Peace into Your Life*. California: Ulysses Press. 2017.

Thompson, Lisa. *Sacred Soul Spaces: Designing Your Personal Oasis*. Washington: Mystic Manta Publishing. 2018.

Virtue, Doreen. *Goddess Guidance Oracle Cards*. California: Hay House, Inc. 2004.

Virtue, Doreen. *Goddesses and Angels*. California: Hay House, Inc. 2005.

Virtue, Doreen and Lukomski, Judith. *Crystal Therapy: How to Heal and Empower Your Life with Crystal Energy*. California: Hay House, Inc., 2005.

Whitbourne, Susan Krauss. "5 Reasons to Clear the Clutter Out of Your Life." Psychology Today, May 13, 2017.

About the Author

D r. Lisa Thompson is a scientist, award-winning interior designer, and Life, Love and Soul Coach specializing in Past Life Regression Therapy and Human Design. She is the author of *Sacred Soul Spaces: Designing Your Personal Oasis*. She is working on her upcoming book, *Sacred Soul Animals: Illuminating Messages and Guidance from Your Spirit Animal Allies*.

Lisa earned a PhD in Organismal Biology and Anatomy from the University of Chicago and was a professor of Biology specializing in anatomy, physiology and evolution of animals. After leaving academia, Lisa followed her passion for interior design and began her business, Design Smart. In her more than ten years in the industry, she has worked with thousands of clients to design and stage their homes and offices.

In June 2017, Lisa trained with Denise Linn and became a certified Advanced Past Life Regression Coach and started her second company, Mystic Manta Coaching. Additionally, she incorporates the tool of Human Design into her life, love and soul coaching practice. She works with clients to create environments that support them physically, emotionally and spiritually, to release blockages and limitations and to access self-love, worthiness and inner wisdom. Through the Past Life Regression process, she connects clients with their deceased loves ones and spiritual messengers and guides.

In working with her clients in the spiritual realm, Lisa has deepened her spiritual awareness and opened up her intuition to a new level of consciousness. She is happily married to the love of her life, Skip, and lives in Olympia, WA with her two children, Nohwa and Curran, two cats, Chana and Bindi, and dog, Jaxx.

Opportunities to Learn More About Sacred Soul Love

FREE meditative journeys and more:

Sign up to gain access to the FREE meditative journeys scripted in this workbook. You will also have access to other information to help you on your journey of revealing and healing your blocks.

Sacred Soul Love: 7 Modules to Manifesting True Love and Happiness by Revealing and Healing Blockages and Limitations:

This online course will guide you through the exercises provided in this book. You will have access to the private Facebook group where you will be among like-minded people going through a similar journey. There will be opportunities to get group coaching via remote live events as well.

VIP Coaching Service:

If you prefer a personal one-on-one experience with Lisa directly, she can coach you through the process of finding true love and happiness, tailored for your specific goals and desires.

For more information, visit:
www.MysticManta.com

Opportunities to Learn More About Sacred Soul Space Design

Sacred Soul Spaces: Designing Your Personal Oasis – the book:

This workbook walks you step-by-step through the design process to create your own personal oasis that nurtures your dreams and goals.

Sacred Soul Spaces: A 7 Module Course to Designing Your Personal Oasis:

This online course will guide you through the design process, with numerous visual examples and explanations to create your Sacred Soul Space. You will gain a more in-depth understanding of how to apply the concepts in your home and office. You will have access to the private Facebook group where you will be able to get help and share experiences with others in the designing process.

VIP Design Service:

If you prefer a personal hands-on experience with Lisa directly, she can help you to design your Sacred Soul Space remotely or in person.

For more information, visit:
www.SacredSoulDesign.com

CPSIA information can be obtained
at www.ICGtesting.com
Printed in the USA
FFHW011620190919
55067350-60792FF